GW00499935

HARRIETTE BROWER IN HER STUDIO

SELF-HELP
IN PIANO STUDY

PRACTICAL LESSONS IN PIANO TECHNIC AND PLAIN TALKS WITH PIANO TEACHERS AND STUDENTS

BY

HARRIETTE BROWER

Author of "Piano Mastery, First and Second Series,"
"Vocal Mastery," "Home Help in Music Study,"
"The Art of the Pianist," etc.

NEW YORK
FREDERICK A. STOKES COMPANY
PUBLISHERS

INTRODUCTION

This sheaf of Practical Lessons in Principles of Piano Playing and Plain Talks to Piano Teachers and Students, have been gathered mainly from the Round Table of *Musical Observer*, with a few culled from *Musical America's* columns. Permission has been granted for their reprinting, in somewhat altered form.

These miniatures are a reflex of the practical working of operative piano teaching and playing. In many cases they are answers to appeals for help from young teachers and anxious students. Some of these and others who have like difficulties, will find their troubles and their problems answered in these brief essays.

If we, as pianists and teachers, are ever to agree on principles of piano playing and teaching; if ever to arrive at a standard based on correct processes, it must be by means of thorough foundational methods, line upon line, precept upon precept. The only things that can, that ought, to be standardized in piano playing and teaching, are the principles which underlie the foundation. These principles appeal first to reason and common sense. When these are in harness the emotions can find expression, not before. The mistake too generally made is to be-

gin at the wrong end, that is with the emotions.
This procedure accounts for much of the uncertainty and chaos in the musical profession.

The author has had unusual opportunity to confer with very many pianists and teachers, some of them of the highest rank. They hold to and advocate the principles brought forward in these pages. These same principles are exemplified in the playing of all the great artists of the keyboard, though only the practiced eye of wide experience may be able to detect and reveal these secrets to the teacher and student.

When it became known to the author that teachers and players thought enough of these stray leaves of precept and advice to gather them up to preserve for personal reference and study, it seemed that a more permanent form might be advisable. This is the prime reason for the collection here offered. The second reason is, as above hinted, the lack of regard for precepts to teach and work by. In either capacity the book may fulfill a humble mission.

HARRIETTE BROWER.

150 West 80th Street,
New York City.

CONTENTS

PART I

PRACTICAL LESSONS IN PIANO TECHNIC

CHAPTER   PAGE

I. THE PRINCIPLES OF PIANO PLAY-
ING 3

II. THE BEGINNER 9

III. TIME KEEPING AND THE TRILL . 14
Time and Rhythm 16

IV. USE OF WRIST AND ARMS . . . 20

V. VARIETY OF TOUCH IN PASSAGE
PLAYING 24

VI. SCALE PLAYING 30

VII. ARPEGGIOS 36
Arpeggios 36
Working Them Out 40

VIII. OCTAVES 42

IX. APPLYING TECHNICAL PRINCI-
PLES TO ETUDES 46
The First Étude 47

X. APPLYING PRINCIPLES TO PIECES 50

v

PART II

PLAIN TALKS WITH PIANO TEACHERS
AND STUDENTS

CHAPTER   PAGE

I. ON TEACHING 57

The Mission of the Piano Teacher . . 57
Are You Prepared to Teach? 59
What is a Good Teacher? 60
Honesty in Music Teaching 62
Examining New Pupils 63
Are You Interesting Your Pupils? . . 64
Teachers' Rights 65
Women Teachers 68
Necessary Courage 69
Two Kinds of Music Teachers . . . 71
Vitalizing the Music 72
How One Teacher Handles Unmusical
   Pupils 74
A Brighter Side of the Woman Question . 75
Be Not Over-Anxious 77
One Teacher's Thought on Experience . 78
Table Work 79
Teaching Bach 81
For the Busy Teacher 83
Handling New Pupils 84
Is Love of Music Impaired by Correct
   Schooling in Music? 86
The City versus the Country Teacher . 89

II. LAYING THE FOUNDATION . . . 91

How One Musical Educator Begins . . 91
Is a Thorough Foundation Necessary? . 98
The Practical Side of a Thorough Founda-
   tion 100
Artistic Movements in Piano Playing . . 101

CHAPTER		PAGE
III.	POINTS ON TECHNICAL TRAINING	104
	Slow versus Quick Finger Movements	104
	A Question of Stiffness	105
	Weak Thumbs	107
	Overcoming Stiffness	108
	Excessive Relaxation	108
	The Question of Relaxed Weight	110
	Weak Finger-Joints	111
	An Outward Sign of Relaxation	113
	Left Hand Study	114
	The Wrong End of Relaxation	116
	The Glissando	117
IV.	THE STUDY OF RHYTHM	119
	The Lack of Rhythm Sense	119
	Playing in Time	120
	A Metronome in Your Head	120
	Beating Time with the Foot	121
	Necessity of Counting, and Counting Aloud	122
	The Count Again	123
V.	TOUCH AND TONE	125
	Getting Results with Tone	125
	Tone Production on the Piano	127
	What Is the Matter with Your Touch?	128
	The Fashion of It	129
	"Playing with Style"	131
	Cultivating Touch	134
	Tonal Perspective in Piano Playing	135
	Principles Applied	137
	Speak with Conviction	139
VI.	ON MEMORIZING	140
	Learning by Heart	140

CHAPTER   PAGE

How do You Memorize Your Program? . 141
Shall Young Pupils Memorize? . . . 143

VII.   FOR PIANO STUDENTS 145
Why do You Study Music? 145
That Unknown Thumb Joint 146
What the Pupil Should do for Himself . 147
"Lend Me Your Ears" 148
Cure for the Stopping Habit . . . 149
Shall We Have Slow or Fast Practice? . 151
Asking Questions 152
A Lurking Danger 153
A Word to the Boys 154
How Much Practice? 156
Playing for Others 157
Be Ready 158
What Constitutes an Artist? . . . 159
An Interesting Letter 161
Hands Above the Keyboard 165
Necessity for Sight Reading 166
Finding a Melody 167
Music Study for the Business Girl . . 168

VIII. POINTS FOR PARENTS TO THINK
OF 170
How Parents Can Help 170
Music in the Home 171
Looking Ahead 173
A Couple of Hints to Parents . . . 174
An Appeal 175

IX.   QUESTIONS AND ANSWERS . . . 177
Age and Music Study 177
Am I Too Old? 178
Teaching Scales 179

CHAPTER   PAGE

When to Teach Scales 180
Scale Playing 181
The Arm in Playing 183
Dishonest Pupils 184
Weak Finger-Joints 187
A Question of "Loose" Knuckles . . . 188
Straightened Fingers 189
Self Education 190
From a Self-Taught Student 193
How Shall I Establish Myself in a Music
    Center? 195

X. IN THE PROFESSOR'S STUDIO . . 199
    The New Season 199
    Appraising the Pupils 204
    Preparing the Hands of a Pianist . . 207
    The Student Musicale 212
    Treatment of the Pupils 215
    Enrollment Day 218
    The Professor Hits Out 222
    The Professor Hits Out Again . . 226

PART I

PRACTICAL LESSONS IN PIANO TECHNIC

SELF-HELP IN PIANO STUDY

CHAPTER I

THE PRINCIPLES OF PIANO PLAYING

THE Art of Piano Playing has been described as " taking and leaving the right key at the right time and in the right way." That is all there is to it! Even though the player has consummate mastery of the instrument and can put into his performance a lifetime of experience and emotion, still the result can be narrowed down to that brief sentence : " taking and leaving the right key at the right time and in the right way." It sounds simple enough : why can we not all do it? Why cannot all those who truly desire to become pianists follow these simple rules and attain what they long for?

The principles governing piano technic are not many, but they must be understood, mastered and followed. Tone production, dynamics, variety of touch are all the results of a knowledge of fundamental laws. Their understanding and practice will form a foundation of the sort which is absolutely necessary if one wishes to acquire an artistic technic and the ability to interpret expressively.

3

The great lack among piano students and young teachers is the lack of efficient preparation. Too often technical principles are not taught or understood; therefore, the playing is slovenly and ineffective. Much is written on this subject, at the present time, in the musical magazines. Some writers, from lack of understanding, shoot wide of the mark, while others express excellent views and give much good advice. But in spite of wise maxims and good advice, indifferent teaching continues, and the failure to grasp the fundamentals of teaching and playing, also the failure to lay a thorough foundation for the student, is paramount.

This lamentable condition of things is constantly brought home to the writer through examination of new pupils and in coaching pianistic classes. In the average class containing a dozen young teachers and players, perhaps not even one may be able to place the hand on the keyboard with correct hand and arm position, and play five keys with correct condition and exact finger action. Such a statement may seem almost incredible, but it is true and has been proved over and over again. Principles of touch and technic are not in the least understood in many instances, even though the player may attempt to perform a Liszt Rhapsodie.

The writer has for years been doing her share — indeed her level best — to combat and improve these conditions, to correct the many errors due to careless early training and to plant the feet

of students firmly on the foundation of the principles of truth. It has now occurred to her that
a larger circle of teachers and students than
those who come under her personal supervision,
might be helped and encouraged to examine themselves and measure up their attainments, if the
essential principles could be plainly set down.

And even a larger public, those who love music
and would delight to take up its serious study,
but who have been obliged heretofore to forego
that pleasure, may be able to start their music
study through following these suggestions, rules
and illustrations.

To all these we offer a series of Lesson Talks
on music study, designed as a means of self-help
in the understanding of essentials of technic.
They must necessarily be brief, but the aim will
be to make them clear and practical — so clear
that "he who runs may read."

The sources of enlightenment about the principles of piano playing come from many directions. From artist teachers, from listening to
and observing the work of the greatest soloists,
and last, but in no way least, from personal analysis and discovery. An artist-teacher like Dr.
William Mason has left a legacy of illustration.
An educator like A. K. Virgil has earned the
gratitude of every student of the piano for the
wonderful work he has done in making clear
what are true principles of foundational technic.
Some of the illustrations of our Talks will follow
along the path blazed by this latter pioneer

standard-bearer for thorough foundational preparation.

It was said a moment ago that there are but few foundation principles. So much the better; they can be the more easily learned. The paramount idea should be to eliminate what is unnecessary and to make extremely clear what is essential; to cast aside material which is superfluous and use only that which gives the kernel of the principle.

Does it ever occur to the student who spends daily hours over masses of études, that he may not be on the right track after all? He believes he is mastering piano technic in the surest manner possible, while he may be very far from the road to it. If he lacks a comprehension of first principles, he will not acquire them by merely rushing through many difficult études and pieces. A thorough and progressive teacher who always insisted on laying a careful foundation for her pupils, affirmed that students always wanted this, *in the end*. At first they sometimes object to the idea of being " put back." But when they realized the benefit of foundational work, they always came back for more, until finally they were willing to " make over the beginning," as they became awake to its necessity.

Why not start right in the beginning? That would surely be common sense. Is it wisdom to spend time and money on the wrong thing? If we do, it can be no surprise to us if we fail to succeed. No, the way of wisdom lies in beginning right, in making a correct start.

In the following Talks, we shall make the directions very clear and simple. The one thing required of the learner will be Thought. To some this may seem the hardest thing of all. It is said the most difficult learning in the world is learning to think. To do anything well requires thinking. The wide-awake teacher, student or music lover knows he must think clearly, knows he must train his mental powers, so he welcomes whatever will lead most surely to this end. You wish to save time, to succeed in what you start out to accomplish and to prove your efficiency. Then you need to train your mental powers from the very start.

The main reason why there are so many indifferent and ineffective players, is because they try to do their work without thinking and reasoning. Young teachers begin the work of instruction without any plan or idea of essential principles; they follow in the old rut, paved and hedged in by old fogyism. A clear idea — a working idea — of a few basic principles is worth all the études in the world. But you must be awake to see this — you must Think and Listen!

As has been remarked the Lesson Talks are designed as a means of self-help in the study of the piano. Even if you have never played the piano, and know nothing more than the notes on the keyboard, you should be able to master foundational principles from directions which will be given.   These must be explicitly followed. They have helped many to obtain a working knowledge of how to master the keyboard: they will do as much for you.

CHAPTER II

THE BEGINNER

A GREAT pianist has said that the player's artistic bank account upon which he should be able to draw at any moment is his technic. Our first business, then, will be to lay the foundation of a reliable, practical, positive technic, a technic upon which we can build a fair superstructure of intelligent, honest playing. The four corner stones of this building shall be — Sincerity, Earnestness, Intelligence and Application.

There are three important principles that will form the basis of our first lesson, and they are: Condition, Position, and Action.

Condition. We must learn how to relax arms, hands and fingers, and then how to render the fingers firm and dependable; wrists must also be relaxed, as it is proved daily that beautiful runs, trills and fine passage work at the piano cannot be done effectively with stiff wrists. Wrists need never be stiff if we start right.

Exercise I. Our first exercise shall be a standing one. Take an easy position with weight on the balls of the feet. Raise the right arm slowly and extend it horizontally, with hand hanging limp from the wrist. Hold this position for five counts, then put the feeling of the rest into the

9

arm and it will fall limply from the shoulder.
If properly relaxed the arm will rebound slightly
once or twice. After several such movements
with the right arm repeat the same exercise with
the left, and then with both together. A second
form of the exercise is to move the hand up and
down for eight counts — while the arm is extended — at the ninth count the arm should fall
relaxed and limp at the side. Repeat the hand
exercise with left arm and hand, then with both
together. These exercises, together with simple
breathing exercises, may be taken night and
morning: always breathe fresh air. Correct
breathing has much to do with good piano playing.

Position. A correct body position is very important. Use a chair at the piano, rather than
the ordinary piano stool, which is apt to be an
uncomfortable affair, and sit so that the elbow is
slightly lower — never higher — than the wrist.
Sit far enough from the keyboard to have the
knees just a little under the edge, then incline
the body slightly toward the instrument — for
you love it! Some beginners crowd so close to
the piano as to almost disappear under it, and
then lean backward — a very faulty position.

*Correct Position of Arms, Hands and Fin-
gers.* The arm should hang free from the shoulder, the outside of the forearm to form a straight
line to middle joint of fifth finger, the wrist loose
and low: the hand assumes a somewhat vaulted
arch at the knuckles, its highest point. The

fifth finger side of hand is well elevated and the two visible joints of the thumb are to be well rounded, while all the fingers keep a curved position.

Action. We will now be seated at a table in order to study finger action. Rest hand and forearm on the table in a relaxed condition. Notice the third or knuckle joint of the thumb is at its base. This is a point generally overlooked among teachers and players. Now draw the finger tips inward, which will elevate the hand to a playing position. The knuckles are now the highest points, from which the hand slopes down to the wrist. If the hand is small and stiff it should be massaged and rubbed for a few moments several times daily, as follows: Stretch the fingers apart, work or bend them back and forth at the knuckle joint; draw the thumb out from the hand and rub the ligaments between the fingers with the thumb and forefinger of the other hand. Such exercises are of great benefit to all kinds of hands — to the large flabby ones as well as to the small, weak ones.

With the hand properly shaped, and the arm still resting on the table, we are ready for finger action. Play the following exercise slowly, with quick, easy motions of the fingers, raising them about an inch and a quarter above the table and always keeping them well curved.

(The figures, up to ten, are the counts; the small figures, above and below the large ones, are for the fingers, up or down).

1   1   1   1   1

Exercise One :   1 2 3 4 5 6 7 8 9 10:

1   1   1   1   1

Each finger in turn is exercised with up and down movements just as the thumb has been. This exercise develops the up-movement of the fingers, a point often neglected at the start.

1   1   1   1   2

Exercise Two :   1 2 3 4 5 6 7 8 9 10:

1   1   1   1   1

(Raise all fingers from the table except the second; play the thumb down at " one " and up at " two."   At " ten " the thumb becomes the supporting finger.)

Each finger in turn is now exercised with the down and up movements, continuing the example set by the first finger.

2 1 2 1 2 1 2 1

Exercise Three :   a: 1 2 3 4 5 6 7 8:

1 2 1 2 1 2 1 3

3 2 3 2 3 2 3 2   4 3 4 3 4 3 4 3

b:1 2 3 4 5 6 7 8:   c: 1 2 3 4 5 6 7 8:

2 3 2 3 2 3 2 4   3 4 3 4 3 4 3 5

5   4   5   4   5   4   5   4

d: 1   2   3   4   5   6   7   8:

4   5   4   5   4   5   4   2

The second finger is again the supporting one. We now play two fingers at the same instant — one down, the other up. If a perfect down and a perfect up motion can be made, they should be correct when put together, and we thus obtain a perfect legato or connected touch. Exercises One and Two are here only written for one finger; they are to be played with each finger in turn. Exercise Three is to be played with each pair of fingers in turn, always returning to the second as the supporting finger, if repetition is desired.

Training the Ear. It is surprising how few there are even among the people who play the piano a little who really hear the tones they play. Many cannot tell a half-step from a whole-step, or a major chord from a minor chord, without looking at the keyboard. It is an easy matter to cultivate the ear by a little intelligent daily practice. Select the octave from middle C to the next C above. Play slowly with one finger and listen carefully. Note the white half-steps, from E to F, and from B to C. Sing or hum these eight tones, first with the piano, then without. Play middle C again, and try to hum any other tone in the octave. This may be a little difficult at first, but if persisted in regularly, a few times each day, a great deal may be accomplished in a short time.

CHAPTER III

TIME KEEPING AND THE TRILL

In our first lesson we got some idea of the bodily and physical conditions necessary for good piano playing; we also learned what are correct positions for body, arms, hands and fingers. With position and condition properly adjusted we began to study finger action in two simple exercises of ten counts for each finger, five up motions and five down motions. If the up and down finger movements are correct we ought to be able to play a perfect *legato* — that is, a perfect connection between the tones when two or more are played in succession. The pivotal point of good finger action for legato passage playing is at the first, or knuckle joint. By "passage playing" is meant runs, scales and arpeggios, in other words, the coloratural of the pianist.

I would suggest here that the student write out in full such exercises as are given from time to time, for this will serve to make the subject clearer. Those already indicated in the first lesson are to be played each hand alone with arm resting on the table; then with hands at the edge of the table, and afterwards at the piano, hands separately and together. The legato exercise, Number Four, is more suitable to play on the piano than the other two. Always drop the hand down gently on five keys and raise all fingers to the "up" position except the second before beginning.

Exercise Four:

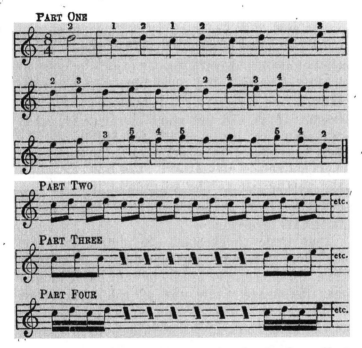

You have played this exercise in single — that is, in quarter notes. After playing the whole exercise through in single notes return to the second finger and begin again, this time playing two notes to a count. These will now be eighth notes. Three notes, or triplets, and four notes, or sixteenths, may be used a little later, when more facility is gained. The exercise will then be built up from one note to two, three and four notes to a count. It will help you very much to write out the whole exercise in notes.

TIME AND RHYTHM

We now come to the study of time and rhythm, one of the most important parts of music. Some people have a natural sense of time, but most of us have to work for it. The place to begin time study is the day we begin music — at the first lesson. If we did not start in this way, when we began, we can correct the trouble now by never playing anything without counting aloud. This should be obligatory. The beat, the count, the rhythm should be so ground into our consciousness from the start that we cannot easily sin in this direction.

That little timekeeper, the metronome, cannot be too strongly recommended. It matters little to the beginner if this or that great pianist has discouraged the use of the metronome. When we have cultivated as perfect a time sense as the artist has, or as he was born with, we, too, can dispense with this tireless monitor. I cannot urge too strongly the constant effort to play in time. It involves not only the ability to play single notes in correct time, but also two, three, four, six or eight notes in the same space of time in which one note is played. In other words, we must have a just sense of the mathematical values of notes. This is only acquired by constant timekeeping and counting.

Another help in our technical study is the practice clavier. The clicks of this instrument will aid the up and down movements of the fingers, and by their means we can know when we are securing a true legato. The metronome can be used with the clavier with much less annoyance than with the piano, velocity and power can be accurately graded, and last, but not least, your neighbors cannot hear what you are doing; therefore, you can practice to your heart's content, and when you are ready with a new piece, which has been studied in private, it can blossom forth at the piano to the delight of your friends and yourself.

As has been already said, a thorough knowledge of note values is necessary to the player, and everything that tends to this end is helpful. Time-beating exercises will accomplish a great deal in this direction. With a loose wrist tap lightly on the table, using the flat end of a lead pencil. Set the metronome at 60, and beat the following exercises:

Exercise Five:

If you cannot beat such an exercise in time it is not likely you can play the notes in time. Various note values can be beaten out in this way, and such exercises will do much to correct a faulty and uncertain sense of rhythm. Rhythm means "measured motion."

Other time-beating exercises may be made by using short pieces of moderate difficulty and tapping the time value of the notes to the beat of the metronome. Easy movements from the Mozart sonatas will furnish abundant material.

A useful gymnastic exercise for increasing the reach between the fingers may be added to this lesson. Sit before the keyboard and place the side of the fifth finger of the right hand on the highest key. Stretch the fourth finger out and put down the farthest key that can be comfortably reached with it. Slip the fifth finger on this key and liberate the fourth which continues to measure off intervals of the utmost distance it can stretch until the middle of keyboard is reached, when the hand is turned in the opposite direction and returns to the top of the keyboard, fifth finger now making the reaches. Left hand begins at the lowest key in the bass with fifth finger, works up to center and back. Right hand now begins at the top with next pair of fingers — fourth and third — after which the third and second may be used. Repeat the exercise in left hand, employing the corresponding pairs of fingers.

Do not neglect the ear-training exercises; give

ten minutes daily to them. Sing the various
tones of the middle octave both consecutively
and by skips. Try to sing a triad, C-E-G, by
merely sounding the lower note of the scale of
one octave. See how many you can sing correctly with only the help of the lowest note.

CHAPTER IV

USE OF WRIST AND ARMS

In our previous lessons we have studied the condition and position of body, hands, arms and fingers. We have made simple up-and-down finger movements with single fingers. When we were sure that these single movements were quick, light and exact, we used each pair of fingers in turn to play a legato trill, with from one to four notes to a count. If in this trill exercise we are making finger movements that are equal and exact, we are acquiring that balance of finger action which is a necessity for a good pianist.

Up to this point we have employed finger touch only, and the fingers have acted solely from the first or knuckle joint.

We will now learn wrist and arm action, with fingers firm at the knuckle joint. It will be seen that this firmness is the opposite principle from the flexibility and suppleness at first joint, which passage playing calls for. We will now test the firmness and strength of the knuckle joint by a pressure, or accent exercise. Sit before the table with hands resting in the lap. Lift arms with hands hanging loosely from wrist, and hold them about seven or eight inches above the table. Now drop hands, with fingers curved,

on the edge of the table. Count eight and at
every beat make a sudden pressure or accent on
the finger tips. This effort will call into play
the triceps muscle in the upper arm. There
must be no bending at any of the joints of the
fingers. At the eighth count raise all fingers to
"up" position except the first. Make the same
accent pressure for each of the seven counts, on
the supporting finger; at the eighth count the
second finger is played and the first is raised.

If the knuckle joints are now strong enough to
withstand this accent pressure without bending,
you are ready to play chords. To play good
chords the fingers must be firm, and those used
for the notes of the chords should be well curved,
and held in such a way as to seem of equal length;
the unemployed fingers should be well raised and
somewhat extended, in order that no extra keys
be struck when the chord is played.

Exercise Six:

Hold the arm above the table, with the hand
drooping as before, the first, third
and fifth fingers curved in readiness to play, the other two fingers
raised and extended. Do not drop
straight down on the chord, but
make an inward movement in the
descent and an outward movement
as the fingers leave the table and
the hand returns to the point
from where it started. In other
words the arm and hand make a rotary move-

ment, and describe an exact oval. The point A is where the hand starts from; the point C is where the chord is played. The arrow indicates the direction of motion. Just as the chord is played the wrist drops, but at once rises and begins to lift the hand with it, to complete the oval movement and reach the point above the table from whence it started. Chords played in this way are likely to be clear, solid and of good tone. This movement gives power and weight to small hands, which without this principle would be able to make but little effect. Practice this chord movement at the table, hands separately and hands together. At the piano begin with the triad C-E-G, and play all the triads of the scale, one on each consecutive key, for two octaves up and back. Repeat in left hand, beginning two octaves below middle C. Always make the rotary movement for each triad, at the same time keeping the hand well arched and the fingers firm. Chords are generally played with more or less of this movement. If the tempo is slow and the theme of the composition dramatic, there will be time and reason for higher motion of the arm; if the tempo is quick there will be only time for a very slight rotary movement; still it should always be present.

The kind of touch we are now using for the chord study is called the " marcato " (sometimes the "half-staccato"). It is indicated by a dot, placed above or below the chord, which means that the chord or note is shortened one half its value. If a quarter note, it will be played as if it were written an eighth followed by an eighth rest.

We have considered only the first position of the triads of C. The other two positions should be practiced just as carefully. The second position in the right hand, E-G-C, and the third position in the left, G-C-E, need the second finger for the middle key.

When we think of the important part played by chords in the making of music, you will see how necessary it is for the player to be able to produce both good tone and variety of touch in chords. Forty years ago, or less, the dramatic value and importance of arm movements in piano playing were not realized. Very little motion of any kind was permitted in the old days. Modern pianism has liberated the arm. You can notice these points when you hear a fine pianist in recital. Rubinstein was, perhaps, the first great artist to show us the wonderful effects that can be made by free arm movements, effects not only of the greatest power, but of the most ravishing quality of tone. Paderewski often plays pianissimo after dropping down onto the keys from a height, with free arm movements.

The chord exercises I have given in this lesson are to be played with the marcato touch. The same should be studied with both the legato and the staccato touches, and their modifications.

CHAPTER V

VARIETY OF TOUCH IN PASSAGE PLAYING

OUR object in these foundational piano lessons, has been to secure correct position and condition of arms, hands and fingers as a first consideration. These principles lie at the bottom of all good piano playing, and it is well-nigh impossible to rear a consistent artistic structure when a good foundation is wanting. Only genius can achieve great results in spite of an ill-prepared foundation.

If the directions have been carefully followed, and the exercises written out and practiced, first at the table, then, if possible, at the clavier, and lastly at the piano, the student should have now acquired quick- and exact up and down finger movements, and should be able to play simple three-voiced chords with firmly prepared fingers and proper arm movements. Many students have studied the instrument for years, yet have not had these fundamentals laid before them and thoroughly explained at the outset.

Command of different kinds of touch is a necessity for the pianist, and a simple exercise in variety can be used by the beginner as soon as he has a clear working knowledge of the legato touch.

Legato means "to bind," and is used for all tones intended to be perfectly connected. Keys should be neither overlapped nor separated.

The *binding*, or *legato* touch is indicated by a line over the notes to be so played. *Marcato* is indicated by a dot placed above or below the note — and the note thus marked is held but half its value. *Staccato*, is indicated by a point above or below the note, and its effect is to shorten the note three-quarters of its value.

The following little exercise will illustrate these three touches.

Exercise 7,

We will now begin the study of passage work, which will lead us to scale playing.

To start with, we must have a clear idea of what is meant by "relation"— relation of fingers, hands and arms to the keyboard. "Five finger relation" is taken when the line of the knuckle joints is on a line with the edge of the keyboard, and the hand is not turned nor slanted either outward or inward. This relation can as

well be preserved when the hands are playing at
either end of the keyboard as when they are occupied in the center of the instrument. The
wrist is the adjuster in every case — and the adjustment will be correct only when the condition
of wrist is loose and unconstrained.

In order to understand and put in practice the
principle of relation, let the student be seated
at the table, and place the left hand upon it, and
in front of the body — with fingers properly
curved, in the position we have learned to know
as the correct and normal one. Put no pressure
on the finger tips. Slide the hand along the edge
of the table and away from the body, for a distance of, perhaps sixteen inches, but do not
change its relation to the edge of the table. It
will be seen that, to keep the knuckles parallel
with the edge of the table, the wrist must be absolutely supple and unconstrained, so that it will
yield to the movement of the hand and arm.
Make several outward and return movements
with left hand and arm; then place the right
hand in position, and go through the same exercise. Now place both hands upon the table
in front of the body, and slide them outward,
away from the center and then return to it, not-
ing carefully how the wrist yields to the easy
steady movement of hands and arms. The body
also aids in this adjustment. For at the outset
of our study, we saw that the body should not be
held stiffly upright, but should incline slightly
toward table or keyboard, so, when the hands are

playing at each end of the keyboard, and are four or five octaves apart — the body yields yet more, and inclines further forward, which aids the hands and arms in taking and retaining an easy and correct relation and position.

Since in passage and scale playing, we no longer keep the hand stationary, but move it up and down the keyboard, we must learn to pass the hand over the thumb, and the thumb under the hand with quickness and adroitness, and in such a way as to preserve the proper position of hand and arm, and at the same time make exact finger movements.

In order to acquire facility in both these principles of action, the following exercise may be practiced.

Exercise 8,

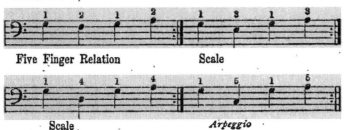

Five Finger Relation   Scale

Scale   *Arpeggio*

(Repeat each measure four times.)

The first and second measures illustrate five-finger relation of hands to keys. (The second can also be used for scale.) In the first measure, at count three, the thumb must not only come down with normal stroke on its key, but the hand must be carried over the thumb with an easy swing, all four fingers being in "up" position. At the fourth beat, the second finger plays the key at the right side of the thumb, which has now been raised to up position under the hand. At the first beat of same measure — when repeated — the thumb plays the note, and the hand is carried back, at the same instant, to its first position.

By this simple means, we demonstrate that the hand can be carried over the thumb (called "*forward motion,*") and carried back from the thumb, (called "*backward motion*") without disturbing the relation of hands to the keys, nor interfering with the pure finger action necessary to produce a smooth even tone.

The second measure is played exactly as the first, except that the third finger is employed, and the hand turned very slightly.

For the third measure, it will be found that the fourth finger will not reach its key if the hand moves over the thumb in five-finger relation: therefore the hand must be turned so that it will assume a slanting position over the keyboard. *Now* it is very easy for the fourth finger to play the key at the right of the thumb, with correct up and down motion.

For the fourth measure, the hand must be slanted yet more across the keys, in order to aid the fifth finger in reaching its key, at the right side of the thumb. In these two measures, then, we have the foundation of scale and arpeggio playing. Arpeggios are simply broken chords.

Practice this little exercise with each hand. The understanding of the principle contained in it will make scales and arpeggios comparatively easy. There is no reason for playing uneven, slipshod scales, where the hand is constantly twisted about, the thumbs are stiff and unmanageable, always playing louder than the other fingers, if these simple rules are understood and followed.

CHAPTER VI

SCALE PLAYING

IN our last lesson we considered the subject of the relation of our hands to keys. We found that "five finger relation," means that the knuckles should be held parallel with the keyboard, while for "scale playing" the hand must be somewhat slanted across the keys, and considerably more slanted for "arpeggio relation." This relation is the same at any part of the keyboard — it being maintained by the flexible adjustment of the wrist.

In order to put this principle into further practice, two exercises are here given, for the development of good touch and fluency in passage playing. Begin with left hand, two octaves below middle C, and play forward four octaves, continuing the figure of the exercise as indicated. Drop fifth finger of right hand on topmost note, and play back to starting point. Both "five finger" and "scale" adjustment of hands to keys may be used.

Exercise 9. 2nd finger crossing over thumb with combined hand and arm movement.

Exercise 9. Left hand. 2nd finger crossing.

Exercise 10. 3rd finger crossing.

Exercise 11. Left hand. 4th finger crossing.

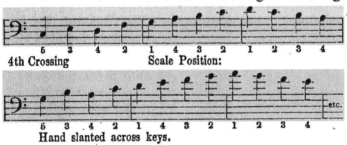

4th Crossing   Scale Position:

Hand slanted across keys.

One of the " five points of technic " is the scale, and scales form a most important part of piano playing. A clear, smooth, flowing, beautiful scale, each note pure as a pearl, is delightful to listen to. A perfect scale cannot be acquired without taking each step leading up to it, in logical order; first, perfect balance of finger action with each pair of fingers; then perfect legato touch in simple five finger exercises; then adjustment of hands, arms and fingers in more extended passages, and finally the scale itself,

Scale means a ladder of tones. Briefly there are twelve major scales, one formed on each of the twelve keys we have. The formation is very simple, as all scales follow the order of intervals found in the model key of C.

Let us consider for a moment our pattern scale, from middle C to the C next above it. It will be seen that between the third and fourth tones, E and F, and between the seventh and eighth tones, B and C, there is but a half stop. All major scales are made after this model. The tone upon which the scale starts is called the keynote, or Tonic. The fifth note of the scale is called the Dominant. Each new scale starts on the dominant of the scale preceding it. Writing out the scales in regular progressive order of sharps and flats will be very helpful to those wishing to have a thorough knowledge of scale formation. For mental training the letters contained in each scale should be recited up and back. This little

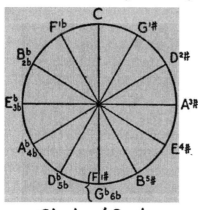

Circle of Scales

diagram of the circle of scales gives the learner a bird's-eye view over the field of scales.

In studying the scale, practice each hand alone at first, beginning with the forward motion.

Sit before the center of the keyboard, and raising left arm with easy, graceful action, hand hanging loosely from wrist, drop, with fifth finger on C, two octaves below middle C. The hand is, of course, held in the slanting position termed "scale relation." Play very slowly, and observe that at A, the hand carries the third finger over the thumb, while at the following D, it is the fourth finger that crosses the thumb. Proceed thus up the keyboard for four octaves (two octaves above middle C). The right arm is now raised, and drops with easy motion, the fifth finger playing the upper C. This descending scale is also in forward motion, because we are moving the hand over the thumb. The same relation of hands to keys should be preserved the whole length of the four octaves, and the crossing movements must be made without disturbing the continuous forward movement of hand and arm, nor interfere with exact finger action.

For the backward scale, use the right hand, and drop the thumb on the lower C, and play slowly up the four octaves to the upper C, which is taken by the fifth finger. The left arm is meanwhile raised, the hand hanging loosely from the wrist, and it drops with second finger on B, then proceeds backward down to lower C. The motion is now away from the thumb. For this reason it is called backward motion. The hand is held slanting over the keys, while the thumb spends most of its time under the hand, being held there as soon as released from its key.

I have endeavored to make these directions as simple and clear as possible. They contain the recipe for correct scale playing. Every one can acquire a beautiful scale who is willing to work for it.

When the principles are understood, and a smooth perfect scale can be played in quarter notes, with metronome at 72, then increase gradually, until 144 is reached. Return to 72 and play two-eighth notes to a beat. When these can be played at 144, set the indicator back to 72 and add sixteenth notes four to a beat. Continually alternate the values of quarter, eighth and sixteenth notes.

Do not be satisfied with your scale until it is perfectly smooth and flowing in sixteenth notes, with metronome at 200. And this is a small part of what may be accomplished, for there seems to be no end to what may be done with scales. You should be able to play as good a staccato scale as a legato one. When you have some control over these two touches, there are modifications of these and other touches to be studied. There is an infinite variety of shadings that may be put into a scale, to make it speak. It must laugh sometimes, and be crisp and gay; it must rise and fall with crescendo and diminuendo, like the wind in the treetops; it must thunder and roar sometimes, like the sea in a storm. You should command all gradations of fineness and force, from the softest whisper up to the greatest power. With proper study, these opposite points will grow farther and farther apart.

A crescendo scale can begin with the softest pianissimo on the lowest note, and increase in force, note by note, until the upper C is reached, which should be the highest point of power. Then return to lower C, with diminuendo, each tone a shade softer than the one before it. Also play the whole scale with equal power, and re-peat with a whispering pianissimo.

Accents are of great value when applied to scales. The principle of the arm accent has already been explained. Each beat — every other beat — and the first beat of every measure may be accented.

When the schoolgirl or amateur speaks with repugnance of scale practice, it is usually because the matter has not been intelligently presented nor studied. Scale playing, as outlined in this lesson, can only prove a delightful and fascinating part of piano study.

CHAPTER VII

ARPEGGIOS

IN these piano lessons we have begun at the very beginning, our aim being to give the principles of piano technic in a nutshell, to give them so clearly and concisely that a beginner with no knowledge of music or the instrument, can start his studies, and make progress through following the exercises and explanations.

Of the five points of our technical star, we have described and exemplified three — namely, Trills, Chords and Scales. The remaining two, Arpeggios and Octaves, will be briefly treated in the two following lessons.

ARPEGGIOS

For scale playing it was explained and demonstrated that the hand must be slanted obliquely across the keys, in order that, when the hand made the necessary crossing over the thumb, the fourth finger could make the proper up and down stroke. This required scale relation of hands to keys. For arpeggio, or broken chord playing, the hand must slant even more obliquely across the keys. The slant must be sufficient to enable the player to put the fifth finger over the thumb, because the fourth is required for the next key but one. Small hands with short fingers are obliged to slant more than large hands with long fingers. This slant must be maintained through the entire four octave arpeggio scale, which we shall study. It means starting the slant with the very first note in the bass, not waiting till the second octave is reached before beginning the slant, as the student is apt to do, unless watching very carefully. For practice in this oblique position of hand, the following exercise will be found helpful in illustrating the point:

Exercise 12.

For the " grand arpeggio," as it is called, we will use three chords: the common triad of C — C. E. G.; the Dom. 7th — C. E. G. B♭.; and the diminished seventh, on C sharp, these three chords, with the correct fingering, and in their broken position, will be seen from the following examples:

Example 13.

Triad of C.   Forward

Dom. 7th.

Dim. 7th.

Example 14.

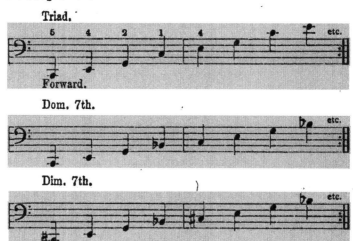

The left hand plays *forward* up four octaves, and the right hand plays down, four octaves, in each of the examples given.

For the backward arpeggio, the right hand starts on the lowest note, and plays up four octaves, when the left hand joins (on G), and returns to the lowest note. These arpeggios are to be played with the legato touch.

If the proper slant and correct relation of hands to keys is preserved throughout, a smooth, even arpeggio with unconstrained movements and good tone will be the result. The difficulty in arpeggio playing, is to get the fourth finger over the thumb, without making a break. Some teachers permit a disjointed arpeggio, and fail to insist on the legato touch. This we cannot condemn too strongly. A smooth, flowing, even arpeggio, perfect in the three chords of each key, and in all keys, is as important to the pianist as is a beautiful scale. With the hand in correct relation, and a flexible thumb, perfection can be approached. To cultivate flexibility of the thumb at the knuckle joint is even more necessary for the arpeggio than for the scale, as the thumb has farther to reach for the arpeggio than in the scale. To tip the hand somewhat toward the thumb when playing arpeggios is an aid in keeping the correct position and relation.

It will be discovered by the thoughtful student when playing these arpeggios slowly forward and analyzing the movements, that the second finger can assist the thumb very much in reaching its key. It should act as a pivot, a feeder, to push the hand forward — ever on, over the thumb. It is through tipping the hand toward the thumb, that the action just described for the second finger is made feasible and possible. With this position of the second finger, it will be seen that the finger does not play exactly on the tip, but rather on the side of the tip. As space will not permit drawings of the various hand positions, I must draw them for you in words, and I have tried to make them as clear and concise as possible.

WORKING THEM OUT

When the forward form of arpeggio scale is somewhat under control, and can be played in quarter and eighth notes at about 72–80, we can attempt the backward form. This is a little more difficult, for, instead of pushing the hand forward over the thumb, we draw it backward, with the thumb held continually under the hand. The position and slant of the hand are exactly the same as in the forward arpeggio, but the principle of pushing is replaced by the backward pull. There are really but few points to remember in the backward arpeggio. With these well in mind, smoothness and velocity can be attained. If any or all of them are neglected there is no hope of securing a smooth, beautiful arpeggio, no matter how many repetitions are made. Two principles must be in mind when studying the backward arpeggio; the slant of the hand and the watchfulness of the thumb, which, like a sentinel on guard, is always held across the palm of the hand, ready to play its key at the right instant and then to return to its hiding place.

As the backward arpeggio is more difficult to reach with smoothness than the forward form, it will require more careful study. When both can be played in quarter and eighth notes at MM–100, try hands together. The left will now play forward, while the right is playing backward at the same time; the first is pushing the other is drawing back. The hands, of course, are slanted in opposite directions. Play slowly, in quarter notes, and increase tempo gradually.

To sum up: The requirements for arpeggio playing are: slant and tip of the hand, pliant thumb; legato touch; constant pushing hand forward on second finger, or pulling it back from second finger.

A smooth, flowing arpeggio — rapid and legato — can only result from slow, careful, intelligent practice. But it is worth working for. It is one of the five cardinal points of technic.

CHAPTER VIII

OCTAVES

THE fifth and last technical point to be discussed is the Octave. The principles involved in octave playing are: loose wrist, arched hand, and firm thumb and fifth finger. Small hands may have trouble with the octave span, but much can be done to obviate this difficulty by stretching the fingers apart, and also by using the massage and gymnastic exercises already suggested in the earlier lessons. Also pulling and drawing out the thumb when it is short, tight and bound to the hand. The thumb is usually an unruly member in any case and needs extra care and watching.

As only two tones are concerned in forming the octave, they can be cultivated by special exercises. The lower tone lends weight and sonority, while the upper tone gives brilliancy to the octave. They should be equal in power; neither should predominate over the other.

As a preliminary to octave study, let us first make movements with arched hand and fifth finger held firmly in place, in a straighter position than the other fingers, which assume meanwhile more of a " stroke position " attitude. The hand

42

action is from a flexible wrist, with quiet arm. Now, with hand and finger in this position and condition, make a number of depressions of the key C — say 4, 6 or 8; then repeat the same movements on D, and so on up the keyboard for two octaves and back. The right hand may repeat the exercise with the thumb, starting on C, two octaves higher up. The left hand now studies the upper note of its octave by repeating the form just played by the fifth finger; also the right hand in turn plays the figure with the fifth finger an octave higher than had been played by its thumb. These movements will render the first and fifth fingers firm, while the hand makes its up and down movements, swinging at the wrist, and the arm accommodates itself by moving slowly up and down the keyboard, as the fingers depress the keys.

Octave scales may now be practiced, first with the lower note and for the distance of two octaves up and back; the left hand using the fifth finger only, and the right hand the thumb exclusively, and afterward the hands together. The upper note may be played in the same manner and for the same distance, first separately and then together, using the thumb only for the left and fifth finger for the right hand.

The octave, thus carefully prepared, may then be practiced each hand alone and afterward using both hands. Staccato touch should first be employed, the arm always hanging freely from the shoulder and moving lightly along with each note or octave played. Quarter notes should be first attempted, and as facility and fluency are gained, eighths and later sixteenths are used, which should finally attain a velocity of MM 120 and more. Small hands should practice these same exercises with a span of six notes, instead of eight, making the interval E to C.

After gaining some control of the two octave scale (in double octaves) a longer one may be studied, in three or four octave length, using the three note values as before.

Legato octaves are very useful and often occur in pieces, generally in slower tempo than the staccato variety. The idea in studying these is to connect the tones by using the fourth finger on black keys and the fifth finger on white keys. Since the black keys are on a higher level and require the hand to be placed a little farther " in " on the keyboard, it will be seen that the wrist naturally rises of its own accord when the fourth finger depresses a black key. If we utilize this tendency, we have an easy, vibrating movement of the wrist, which is depressed when the white keys are played and elevated when black ones are used.

Let the right hand put this elevating and lowering principle into operation by playing a one-octave scale — chromatically and in octaves. The first note, C sharp, requires an elevated wrist, and so on up the scale.

Correct octave practice develops strength of wrists and arms, gives firmness to the first and fifth fingers, and therefore to the whole hand. It should be employed much more than it is by the player in the early stages, as the control acquired is helpful to the remaining technical points; in fact, each point helps the other.

As we have now gained the principles of finger movements, illustrated by legato in the trill and simple scale passages, of arm movements in chords, of scale and arpeggio relation, we must be able to apply these principles when we attempt to study a piece of music. It may have taken us two or three months to acquire the control of fingers, wrists and arms needed for the exercises described in these lessons. But they are worth working for, for they are the foundation principles lying at the beginning of all technical and musical progress. They are never to be cast aside, but are to be always applied.

CHAPTER IX

APPLYING TECHNICAL PRINCIPLES TO ETUDES

WE have been chiefly concerned with the principles of piano technic, in this set of lessons. Principles of finger action have been illustrated by trills, scales, arpeggios and passages; principles of arm weight and arm movement applied to single fingers and chords. We must now learn to use these ideas in études and pieces.

Let it first be understood that we never ignore or give up the principles we have learned with so much care and thought. If they were necessary to learn in order to lay a firm foundation, they are needed all along the course of our progress in piano playing; in fact, they are never laid aside. Some students who have gone over foundational work with creditable diligence, quite fail to apply, in fact, are inclined to lay it aside altogether when they come to study an étude or piece. They seem to think strictness and exactness only belong to the thing called technic, and that when they begin to play pieces they are at liberty to do as they like.

This is an unfortunate error, and doubtless may be at the root of some of the poor piano playing one hears. At all events, it causes the conscientious teacher a great deal of trouble, for she must constantly reiterate the rules and principles taught in the beginning, reminding pupils to carry them out and apply them.

As the student who works out these lessons is his own teacher, we caution him to watch with care, to see that every rule is being carried out in his practice.

THE FIRST ETUDE

The first étude to which we shall apply our foundational knowledge is one by Duvernoy, Op. 120, No. 1. The first five of these short studies are published separately; the student should do at least four, as these illustrate different phases of technic in a simple and pleasing way.

Let us see what we can find in number one. There are many things; in fact, the longer we look at it the more things we may discover. Indeed, it will be better if we sit down away from the piano and consider the printed page before us. First as to the way the little piece is put together. The key is C major, and the right hand plays the one octave scale, beginning on the tonic. In the second measure, the left hand begins on the fifth, or dominant, playing one octave scale also.

These little scale figures continue for seven measures. The four following measures are made up of a simple figure that goes up three notes and down five; then the left hand is added for another four measures. Following this are eight measures of more one octave scales, after which comes a little curved figure of notes, for ten measures, the form of which should be observed. The left hand during these eight measures adds one chord in each. The closing four measures use both hands for scales in both similar and contrary motion. If you will count them you will find there are thirty-eight measures in this étude. You will also see that the right hand, from the seventh to thirty-fourth measures is not once lifted from the keys, but executes a continuous " passage." These few suggestions merely show how to analyze a piece as to plan, how to pick it apart to discover how it is formed. The more we can find out about it, unaided, the easier the effort to learn and remember it will become. If you are able to discover what the various chords are and how related to each other, so much the better.

We will now go back to the beginning and consider how to apply our technical knowledge to the performing of this étude. If the student who is teaching himself to become a player, is able to do some of his practice on a Practice Clavier, his progress will be much more rapid.

For the actual learning of the étude, it is advisable to take a small portion, say eight measures, with each hand alone. See that exact finger movements are used, and correct passing of thumb under hand and hand over thumb, in these one octave scales. Each time they come to an end the hand is lifted by the arm — the wrist starting first — and is held suspended until the moment when it must descend on the next measure. Pure legato touch is required for the scales and everything must be precise and exact. Proceed in the same way, with sections of four or eight measures, played each hand alone, then together, through the piece. The second page contains chords for left hand. Play the succession of eight with legato touch and arm movements. The subsequent phrased pairs of chords must be done with exactness, the large chord taken with prepared fingers and down arm weight, the small one with up arm movement.

We have now subjected the étude to musical and technical analysis. Now comes the working up; the metronome will be needed here. The whole étude can be played through, each hand alone, using four beats to the measure instead of two, that is, four eighth notes, starting at 60. Work these up to 120. When this can be accomplished with absolute smoothness and precision, put the metronome at 60 again and use hands together. We can gain greater speed by working up the tempo to a higher figure, but the student, at this juncture, should not strive for speed at the expense of clearness and precision. The careless player often hurries ahead, heedless of errors. This state of things is difficult to overcome, once it really gains the upper hand. Be willing to " make haste slowly," which pays in the end.

CHAPTER X

APPLYING PRINCIPLES TO PIECES

WE have been told "phrasing is the art of dividing a melody into groups of connected sounds, so as to bring out its greatest musical effect, including accents and dynamics." A musical composition consists of a series of short sections, each more or less complete in itself; it is the mingling of these little blocks of melody and their connection with each other that form a coherent musical story. The phrases, or groups, are like clauses and sentences in a book.

Language and music are closely connected; indeed music is a language, the language of the emotions. Let us never lose sight of this. Reading from a book requires two things — besides clear enunciation — they are accent and punctuation. Just so musical phrasing depends on the stress of the sounds and their connection with or separation from each other. To make music intelligent and meaningful, we must know how to punctuate it, we must make it *speak*.

It will be necessary to learn a few simple definitions and then see how we can apply them. Just as in language, so in music, we have the complete sentence, or period; the half sentence or clause; and the germ thought or little motive.

50

The period makes a complete statement; the phrase is the half statement; the motive is the smallest musical thought; in thematic music it is taken as a musical text. The act of playing these different parts coherently and expressively, so as to make the musical story intelligent to player and listener, is termed phrasing. Thus it would seem the word "phrase" applies to a part of the musical sentence, while the word "phrasing" is the application of the principles of touch and punctuation.

To illustrate this point: Here is an example of a half-period or phrase: "If I go to town to-morrow"— this is quite incomplete and makes no definite statement. When a second phrase or clause is added —"I will buy a new gown," renders the sentence, or period, complete. This is a simple sentence with two clauses. Just so in music; in so-called regular form, a period consists of two phrases, the second answering and completing the first.

In order to learn these things for ourselves, we must try to analyze the music we play, that we may play it intelligently. In taking up a piece, we look first at the signature to find in what key the piece is written, whether in a major or minor mode. When the key is decided, play the seven triads belonging to that key up and back to become more familiar with the material of the key. It is well to recite the notes of these seven chords with the metronome, set at about 80.

Through reciting the triads of the scale we can locate the tonic triad on the keynote, the chord of the sub-dominant on the fourth, and the dominant on the fifth note of the scale. These three triads are the most important in the key.

Now return to the piece in hand and apply the principles of phrasing mentioned above. If the form is what is termed regular, the first phrase will end on the dominant, and the phrase will be likely to contain four measures. But a phrase in music ending on the dominant is only half complete, only half finished. A question has been asked; the second phrase will answer it. Only when this has been done will the period be complete. All this is really very simple, any one can understand it. There is no reason why music pupils should often play the piano for years without an inkling of how to analyze and phrase their music; but alas, this often happens.

The object of phrasing, then, is to render the ideas expressed in the composition clear and intelligent by means of punctuation, accent, variety of touch, also by separating groups of tones through lifting off the hands in a variety of ways. As has been said, in regular form, the phrase contains four measures, the period eight. The classic writers, Bach, Hayden, Mozart, and often Beethoven, wrote according to these rules. Modern music, on the other hand, often departs widely from the section idea, it is not developed block-wise, but frequently is declamatory and rhapsodical. We must learn to punctuate mod-

ern music with equal care, only in a different
way. There will be many marks of phrasing,
but these marks will take the form of variety in
touch and tone.

The two special touches which give variety to
the phrase are the legato and staccato. The
group may be marked like this:

Exercise 15:

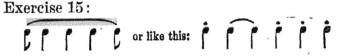

Look through the Fantaisie of Mozart, in D
minor, and note how many kinds of phrasing
there are; one marked

Exercise 16:

seems quite difficult to master. Without careful attention to touch and phrasing, these little
groups of three notes would sound quite monotonous and all alike. Rightly articulated they
are expressive and charming.

The self-made student is advised to now take
up various small pieces as short studies in
phrasing, touch and punctuation. There are
many collections of small pieces; perhaps none
are more delightful than the Album for the
Young, by Robert Schumann. Play the "Little
Piece" for smooth legato; "Soldier's March"
for crisp staccato and clearness; "First Loss"

for sympathetic tone quality; the "Happy Farmer" for melody in left hand, against light marcato chords of accompaniment in the right. Unless the right hand is carefully watched, it is inclined to hold the second chord of each pair too long, thereby giving it accent and undue prominence. This should not be permitted. Then there is the little "Scicillian," which contains a variety of note values and marks; further on we come to the "Romance," which contains again melody and accompaniment, legato and staccato, and so on through the set.

With what we already know of various touches and principles of phrasing, any one should be able to render small pieces like those in the Schumann Album, with accuracy and charm.

PART II

PLAIN TALKS WITH PIANO TEACHERS AND STUDENTS

CHAPTER I

ON TEACHING

THE MISSION OF THE PIANO TEACHER

To my teachers and to all who are giving instruction in music: I wonder if you are awake to the high calling of your profession, to its responsibilities and opportunities? We are often told that the call to teach is the most sacred, the most influential any one can undertake, because of the opportunity it gives to guide and mold young thought and influence young lives. The teacher needs to be high-thoughted and inspiring. If you have risen to this vantage ground, in thought, to this post of honor, you will surely wish to fill it with high ability.

Be sure you have something definite to teach; be sure you understand your subject and know how to present it. You must be filled with the idea that you have the beautiful Art of Music to impart, nay to reveal to others; be filled with it and enthusiastic over it. Only then will your enthusiasm overflow to your students. Without enthusiasm your work will be cold and dead. Of what use is the profoundest theoretical knowledge, coupled with wide musical learning, without the magic touch of enthusiasm to kindle the light in others. To have this enthusiasm, you must love your work — love every bit of it, even the so-called dry details of teaching the rudiments to beginners. To me there is nothing dry or soulless about any of it, not even about the first lessons; for to me the beginning is of absorbing interest, as great as the teaching of the most brilliant solo. There are no little things; every principle is important. If we would only remember this, we would take as lively an interest in presenting the technical steps to piano mastery as in teaching repertoire.

The vital question is: do you know every step of the way you are trying to lead the pupil? Is it the best way, the most advanced in thought, the most logical? Does it bring results?

In the present state of world conditions, the calling of the teacher of music is more important, higher and more sacred, than it ever was before. Music is one of the greatest forces to uplift and cheer. We cannot do without it. Then inspire your pupils with your own enthusiasm. Do more than you have ever done to urge regularity, studiousness, thorough study and enjoyment through music.

Remember your pupils are not only learning the piano and how to play it from you, but they learn many other things besides. That is one reason why you cultivate yourself in all possible ways outside of music. That is why you have need for enthusiasm in your work.

ARE YOU PREPARED TO TEACH?

Said one of the prominent pianists and teachers to me recently:

"Many young players plunge into the work of teaching with but very little preparation — often with no preparation at all. A while ago, one of my students, who at that time had not been with me very long, remarked: 'I should like to begin to teach.' I said: 'Do you think you are ready to teach?'

"'I ought to be, I've been taking lessons for five or six years.'

"'What will you do with a beginner; what will you teach first?' she was asked.

"'I think I would begin with scales.'

"'My dear child, I can see you haven't the faintest idea of how to teach the piano; you ought to be regularly prepared to do it.' The result was she took special pedagogical work in connection with her private lessons for at least a year. At the end of that time she began to teach and is now having remarkable success with young pupils."

How many young pianists, who wish to join the ranks of the profession, are willing to follow the footsteps of this student and systematically prepare for the work? Do not imagine, simply because you have been playing the piano for years, that you are therefore qualified to teach that instrument. It is likely you have left the fundamentals so far behind — if you were really taught them in the beginning — that you have quite forgotten them. Even if you still remember, you must learn how to apply them to different hands and mentalities. You must learn to systematize the foundation in the most up-to-date manner; you must know different ways to illustrate the same principle.

Before undertaking the difficult task of the teacher, examine yourself and consider whether you have the requisite knowledge and equipment. See what you lack, then set about preparing yourself thoroughly for the work. We never know what we can do till we try. Have faith in yourself, back it by sound preparation, love your work and everything connected with it, and you are bound to succeed!

WHAT IS A GOOD TEACHER?

This morning a couple of street musicians halted beneath my window; the man scraped on his fiddle, while his partner drawled a popular ditty in an execrable voice. At the conclusion they called out: "All kinds of music lessons given!" Perhaps some passer-by might be ignorant or foolish enough to want that kind.

We have got to educate the people of this country into taking music seriously. Then the next step will follow naturally; they will want to study it seriously, and will realize they must have good teachers.

What is a good teacher: what must one know to be a good teacher? A teacher worthy the name should be able to lay a good foundation, if the pupil lacks this necessary article. He may prefer to teach interpretation to advanced players, but he ought to know the beginning, so he can diagnose the case and prescribe the correct remedy. This of itself needs wide knowledge and experience. He ought to know how to produce — and teach — mellow tone quality, with different touches and dynamics; he should know good scales, arpeggios, chords and octaves, and how to cultivate them artistically; how to analyze a piece to find its form, harmonic structure and so on. It may be he only professes to know the technical side, not going deeply into interpretation of difficult compositions. Then let him know everything about foundational study, and know it thoroughly. We have the sorest need in this country, at the present moment, for competent teachers of this description. There are many artist teachers with us, to whom Americans flock, for the sake of the name and prestige. But alas, they are not ready to profit by what the artist can give. To have lessons with Mr. A, Mr. B, or Mr. G, will not make them pianists, or good musicians, if they are not prepared for the great pianist's instructions. Of course *he* knows the whole piano literature — *except the beginning, which he has* long ago forgotten. Both these classes of teachers should work together, the foundational instructors and the artist teachers. Then more successful results would follow.

HONESTY IN MUSIC TEACHING

Honesty in music teaching? What an idea! you exclaim. We of all people are strictly honest. Music teachers as a class are a very hard working set of people, who earn little enough for all the labor they expend. Some of us can hardly make ends meet; but above everything else we believe we are honest.

Not quite so fast, my friend. If you were absolutely honest to the pupil, your thorough training would command better fees, for you would be more competent; you would much more than make ends meet.

I fear you may have fallen into a rut, through the routine of lesson-giving; you need to be aroused. Pupils expect new, up-to-date ideas. Are you prepared to give them what they want and are paying for? Are you constantly advancing yourself? Do you study new compositions, attend piano recitals and other concerts, read books on music, and subscribe to musical periodicals? It may be that you do all these things, yet you may not be entirely honest in other ways.

Is it honest, think you, when a new pupil comes, and you see she has been very badly taught, not to tell her where she stands? You see what she needs. You know she ought to drop her brilliant pieces and come right down to the foundation of things. She can never get anywhere while these glaring faults hold her down.

But you fear to tell her the truth. You think you will lose her, that she will go to a more unscrupulous teacher, who will make her fine promises. So you also withhold the truth and feed her on pieces with which she can make a show. Thus you lose your chance to be honest.

But the truth will come out one day. Some one will be more courageous and the girl will learn of your error. In that day you may wish you had been honest, for, after all, "Honesty is the best policy."

EXAMINING NEW PUPILS

In examining new pupils at the beginning of the season, the conscientious teacher has a difficult and at the same time delicate task, to classify them and rightly appraise their mental characteristics, their aptitude, ability and temperament.

The task is, first of all, difficult because the prospective pupil may play quite passably a piece she has worked upon a long time, and deceive you as to her real status. It requires much experience and a practiced eye to detect at once all her weaknesses, her lack of correct principles; it needs more than ordinary insight into human nature to diagnose such a case and apply the needed remedy.

It is also a delicate task because, if the pupil has some little aptitude, yet has never been rightly developed, you don't want to tell her she has been taught "all wrong," and must go back to the beginning. You want to be honest yet you want to use tact, not to antagonize her at the outset.

It is a good plan to ask the applicant for some scales, after she has played her "piece." You thus put the finger — innocently of course — on her weakest spot. Ten to one, though she has just played a Liszt Rhapsodie, she cannot go through the scale of C respectably, even without the metronome; with it would be utter failure. She will see this herself. Then try her on chords; she never thought of doing them outside of pieces. The same results will follow tests of trills, arpeggios, octaves, time beating and ear training. When the new pupil realizes she cannot do these things correctly, she will probably be reconciled to repairing her technical ways, and even ready to rebuild her foundation, if you advise it.

Be tactful, earnest and full of enthusiasm, and you will win the pupil every time.

ARE YOU INTERESTING YOUR PUPILS?

The question of interesting pupils is one which every serious teacher should bring home and strive to answer.

Has your manner of teaching so crystallized that you are treating all pupils alike, putting them through the same methodical grind, giving the same pieces you have used for the past twenty years? If so you have fallen into a rut in your work and need to be aroused out of it.

Realize that all pupils cannot be put through the same method nor play the same pieces. The principles of piano study can be presented from different angles, suited to hands and mentality of each pupil. This is where the insight, experience and intuition of the capable teacher are of highest value; they enable him to decide quickly just how to treat each pupil, what material to give, and so on.

If you would be a successful teacher, you must study the mentality of each pupil. This takes thought, care, much knowledge and experience, but its accomplishment will place you higher in the scale, and render you more efficient.

In order to interest your pupils you do not need to simplify everything and make it childishly easy; on the other hand, do not expect them to believe blindly everything they are told, without having the reasons explained. A well-known teacher said: "I talk to my girls and boys of a dozen years as though they were twenty; I explain principles, the reason they are principles and what they are for; each step, each exercise has its place in the whole scheme. They understand everything as they go along and find the logical working out much more interesting than if I asked them to accept everything on faith, without knowing why."

TEACHERS' RIGHTS

We hear so much about what teachers should do for their pupils. A truly conscientious teacher does all in his power to assist and inspire his pupil, and it is surely a privilege for the pupil to study with a competent, progressive teacher.

It might be well to look at the question from another side and consider what belongs to the teacher; what he has the right to expect and require of the pupil.

A teacher of established reputation has the right to expect a student to take at least twenty lessons. It is very unfair to the teacher to judge his or her work after one or two lessons, or even after five. A music school could be mentioned where a pupil can engage lessons with any of its teachers, with the understanding that he can' change instructors after a lesson or two. The teacher is put on trial, so to say, though most teachers in the school are of recognized ability. The result is that if a new pupil finds the first lesson somewhat exacting and sees that serious study is expected of him, he has the right to leave that teacher at once and try an easier one, with whom he can do more as he pleases.

This is all wrong, you say; the teacher's rights should be respected by that school. The teacher, also, should require the pupil to remain with him a certain length of time. He must stand for his own rights.

The teacher should require every lesson to be paid for, whether taken or not. Neither should he be expected to make up lessons, unless it be his good pleasure to do so. The only way to secure and safeguard the business basis of musical instruction, is to exact payment for the whole, or half term, in advance. When lessons are already paid for, pupils do not ask to be excused on slight provocation.

The teacher expects — especially in the case of young pupils — to have the coöperation of parents, in looking after practice hours and other items connected with their children's music study. He expects there will be sufficient interest in music, in the homes of his pupils, that they shall come to him with well-prepared lessons.

The teacher has a right to expect promptness in everything. Promptness in attendance, promptness in procuring whatever is needed in the way of tools, i.e., music, books, metronome and so on. Also promptness in paying bills.

The earnest teacher, striving to make his work of greatest value as well as pleasure to his pupil, expects the pupil will respond by showing interest in his work, especially in the lesson hour. Nothing dampens the teacher's ardor more than to have pupil sit passive, absorbing like a sponge, without asking a question or saying a word. It is a teacher's privilege to expect cheerful coöperation with his efforts to impart musical knowledge and experience to his students, to aid them by showing interest as well as attention, a desire to aid them by giving his best endeavor in mastering the means of musical expression.

WOMEN TEACHERS

A friend of mine who chanced to recommend a woman piano teacher to a group of people, was met by discouraging comments on women teachers in general. In vain my friend pointed out there are various kinds of women teachers, some quite equal to men. The words fell on deaf ears, for the people held to their own views.

Several causes have brought woman's work along educational musical lines into disrepute. She is thought to lack thoroughness, to have almost no plan of systematic study, to be unable to impart force, power or style. These seem to be the prime reasons, expressed or unexpressed which cause students who lack these points, to go to a man for them.

Why is not the woman teacher thorough? Why can she not impart a forceful style?

For the best reason in the world, because she has not been thoroughly trained herself. If she plays at all, it is in a weak, colorless style, which is designated as " feminine."

This sort of woman teacher never took her music seriously, when she did occupy herself with it. Later, when she needed spending money, or was obliged to support herself, she turned to music-teaching as the easiest way. Her teaching was not taken seriously either. She had always played in a weak, ineffective manner, so it is no wonder her pupils fall into line and imitate her. Teachers of this kind

bring an ill name on all women teachers, which
is more or less of a problem for the competent
teacher to overcome.

Are you one of the teachers who have not laid
a good foundation yourself, who do not continually study and progress, who do not keep up
with the times, who have no special plan of instruction? Your responsibility is great. Realize that while you deprive yourself of the privi-
leges of thorough study, attending recitals, keeping in touch with the world of music through
books and periodicals, you are injuring others;
you are bringing disrepute on the great army of
women teachers, who are capable and progressive.

There are many of these — thank Heaven!
There are many women teachers as capable, yes,
more capable than men. They have as much
knowledge and more tact, patience and intuition.
They can impart as much technical skill, as
much power, freedom and style. They are the
women who constantly study to improve their
work and their own equipment. One such
teacher in any locality is sure to make for good
to all the rest. All honor to her!

NECESSARY COURAGE

A young player went to an artist-teacher for
lessons. After hearing her play, he told her to
prepare a Beethoven Sonata, a Chopin Nocturne
and a salon piece for her first lesson.

Now this young woman had a very meager

technical equipment; her fingers were weak and bending, her tone thin and uncertain, her playing ineffective, as it naturally would be under such conditions. She had no velocity, no decision of touch, no power, resonance or variety of tone. What she really needed was a thorough course of training in technic and tone production. Why did not the artist-teacher tell her the truth and advise such a course? For several reasons.

1. He had not the courage, as he feared he might lose her as a pupil, and she was able to pay his price.

2. He realized he could not give her the technical training she so much needed, yet he did not want to pass her on to a teacher lower down.

3. He thought she should be working on pieces in order to have something to show, and believed she would not be willing to pay his price simply for technical instruction.

For these and other reasons he deemed it more politic to give her pieces at once and keep the truth about her technical deficiencies in the background.

It requires true courage to tell a pupil her faults and then set about correcting them. It requires courage and patience to work with pupils to lay a good foundation, to help them correct their manifold errors, when they have been badly taught, to guard them against discouragement, to spur them to do their best, to ever point them onward and upward.

Have you the necessary courage to tell pupils the truth? Also the necessary knowledge to lay the foundation they need?

TWO KINDS OF MUSIC TEACHERS

There is a certain class of people who claim to teach music, or the piano, rather, who know little or nothing about the subject. Some instances of their methods might be amusing were they not sad commentaries on gross ignorance and indifference. One of these persons, by profession a piano tuner, gives lessons in his unemployed hours. One pupil took his lesson while his teacher sat at supper. The boy played about as he liked, the only correction being for wrong notes, for which the piano tuner would call out to him from the next room. One day the boy awoke to the fact he had learned almost nothing, and had to "begin all over again" with a more conscientious, capable teacher.

Another boy was taught by a so-called professor, who, at the beginning of the lesson would light his pipe, lie back in his chair and dream, rousing once in a while to call out *"falsch!"* when a wrong note was played. Another teacher, a woman this time, used to bring her knitting or embroidery, and work vigorously during the lesson period.

Such cases are impossible, unheard-of, you exclaim. Not at all. They have all come under my notice, and many more of the same sort. Such acts come from ignorant, indifferent teachers. There are still many of them, not only in out-of-the-way places, but in great music centers as well.

We pride ourselves on the rapid advance of musical knowledge in America, and with good reason. Our progress has been marvelous; yet there are still so many dark corners, so much unenlightenment. We beg the teachers who have the light — teachers who know — to let their light shine into the gloomy places and dispel incompetence and sloth.

Real teachers cannot be ignorant or indifferent; they realize their responsibilities. They are wise, resourceful, competent. They adapt their work to the needs of each pupil, though they teach scientific principles to all. They take a deep interest in each student, and, in return, expect thorough, conscientious study.

We rejoice to encourage the efforts of this ever increasing army of capable instructors. By so doing we shall do our share to extinguish the darkness of ignorance and bring in the light of true knowledge and efficiency.

VITALIZING THE MUSIC

" I have no idea how this piece ought to sound," says the anxious pupil.

" Have you learned notes, fingering and phrasing? " asks the teacher.

" I think so; at least I have practiced the piece a great deal, but can't seem to make it mean anything."

A great many pupils are in the same condition. They seem unable to say anything with their fingers — to make the music speak. In fact, few pupils, during their earlier years, are able to make their music expressive or distinctive. They don't know how to get back of the notes, to find out what they mean.

Piano playing means so much more than setting keys in motion! We, teachers of the piano, must use every means to enlighten our pupils as to the significance of whatever they attempt to play. Above all we are to so teach them that they learn how to find out the meaning for themselves.

Why is much of the piano playing done by students so ineffective and meaningless? If the teacher understands why and clearly recognizes what is lacking, faults can be more easily rectified.

Is *Rhythm* lacking? Correct this lack by systematic counting aloud, time beating, use of metronome and study of pieces having well-marked, infectious, rhythmic swing.

Is *Tone* weak and ineffective? Touch must be made clear and distinct; fingers must act freely at knuckle joint, must gain precision and strength.

Does the pupil lack *Color* and *Variety?* He must learn to play simple exercises and scales with shading and expression.

Does the pupil understand principles of *Phrasing?* If not, he must be shown how to analyze his music, find motives, phrases, periods and how to punctuate. He must also study Fingering and Pedaling with great care. If all these factors, necessary to make the music intelligent and expressive, have been thought out and obeyed, the student will bring his piece to the lesson thoughtfully prepared. It will be expressive according to his lights. If the teacher is then able to play it for him as it ought to be played, this will be an added assistance toward vitalizing the music.

HOW ONE TEACHER HANDLES UNMUSICAL PUPILS

Some musical educators claim all pupils are musical, only their perceptions in this particular direction have not been aroused. Be this as it may, some pupils seem well nigh hopeless. One teacher writes:

" Many of my new pupils have come very badly prepared, indeed knowing almost nothing. Among them are two young girls of fourteen. They have been badly taught, by a shiftless teacher. They only take lessons 'to please mother,' and are very lukewarm themselves. The first thing I did was to read duets with them, together with the tapping and counting of time exercises, and explanation of musical signs and terms, for they know little of time or rhythm. Duet playing for the first time teaches them to count aloud, for this I insist on. As they have never had a metronome, they naturally hate it, so I at first only use it in the lessons. You see I must induce them to think, yet not turn them against music at the start. I next select some simple piece, and play it through several times, the pupil tapping the rhythm of the melody, then that of the accompaniment. Next we recite the notes, and finger it, at the table. After this we pick out the notes with one finger, playing as nearly in rhythm as possible. Such pupils have no idea how to study or how to memorize; so first of all I try to make a musical appeal, for this kind of girl is not serious. At first I make no technical demands, for the girl does not even know the word. I only introduce table technic (the kind I begin with) after the child has become interested and has confidence in me. The best way is always to go to the bottom of things and start over, but the drop, in this case, would be too sudden, so I must go slowly."

No doubt this young, earnest teacher is doing right in first gaining the interest and confidence of her pupil. We all prefer pupils who are willing to lay a thorough foundation. But it is a real satisfaction to awaken dormant musical sense and make a good student out of a poor one.

A BRIGHTER SIDE OF THE WOMAN QUESTION

One of my boys is making excellent progress, with which he seems thoroughly pleased. He received a call from a friend lately, who asked him to play and commented most favorably on his performance. He asked who was teaching him, and when he heard it was a woman, remarked: "Why don't you study with a man?"

This simple question reveals the attitude taken by many persons in regard to the sex of the teacher.

In the earlier stages of musical development in America, the woman teacher of music was apt to be a very insignificant person indeed, who generally took up piano teaching in order to have a little spending money. She flourished because, in those days, the prevailing idea was that a cheap teacher was good enough for a beginner. But times have changed; we are advancing rapidly in the appreciation and comprehension of music. We have learned that the beginner requires the most careful and thorough instruction. The woman teacher has been forced to cultivate herself, to make a thorough study of the things she endeavors to teach. No doubt in small towns and villages there are still many of the old sort left; but it is also true there are many excellent women teachers who are using up-to-date methods and are doing splendid work. Such teachers usually locate in the music centers. The very fact that a woman can establish herself in a great metropolis, where competition is so keen, that she can hold her own, make good and earn an excellent income, proves that the American woman teacher has — under certain favorable conditions — come into her own and is a force to be reckoned with.

What do we not owe the faithful, competent woman teacher! Her patience is inexhaustible, her resources ample, her sympathies keen, her interest never failing. In some of these qualities she often far surpasses the man pedagogue, who has little patience with mediocrity and who only wishes to accept talented pupils. She it is who is willing to work with a pupil to correct the endless faults of poor instruction, or to guide the hesitating footsteps of the beginner, till they rest firmly on a strong foundation. She it is who will try to make something out of the untalented pupil, often cast off by the professor.

All honor to the unselfish woman teacher of ability and understanding. She is aiding greatly in America's musical progress, and we owe her support, recognition and gratitude.

BE NOT OVER-ANXIOUS

Are not some of us apt to be over-anxious with our pupils? In the desire to explain everything, to watch everything, are we not doing too much ourselves; do we leave enough for the pupil to do? The pupil must be shown how to help himself; he must be held responsible for his own faults and mistakes.

Then, when the composition is well under way and we ask for a complete performance, are we not prone to direct the performance too minutely? We are familiar with the professor who paces the studio during the playing of the piece, calling out, "loud," "soft," "slower," or "faster"— until the player is well nigh distracted. Occasionally the student is inspired, but more often the opposite effect is produced.

I suggest another course. Study the pupil and his performance in perspective, as it were. Remain quietly observant at the farther end of the studio. Tell the pupil you will be the audience and she must get her effects to you " over the footlights." Watch the result. Do not help her with a single suggestion. Hands off! Let her work it out. Insist on a smooth, even performance, free from mistakes. Let her first show what she can do, then make corrections when she has finished.

When a new piece is taken up, pitfalls may be pointed out, with the best way to master them; at a later stage hear the piece from beginning to end without interruption. This puts the pupil on her mettle; she has no excuse for making mistakes other than her own unfamiliarity with the music. She realizes she must give more time and study. It was Beethoven's idea to play the piece through without interruption, and it is often a good principle to follow.

ONE TEACHER'S THOUGHT ON EXPERIENCE

It is experience that counts every time, in both teaching and playing. As a lad I went through the Well Tempered Clavichord; I analyzed every prelude and fugue, from beginning to end. When I had done that I said: " Now I am through with those." But as time went on and I got a little wiser, I went back to Bach and found there was yet a great deal to learn from those same preludes and fugues. Some of us think we are way beyond Liszt now, at least pupils do, if they play much modern music. But when they grow wiser they will find there are many beauties in Liszt and all the masters before him, which they have not yet discovered.

Another thing. One may play all the notes of a piece correctly; every sign and expression mark may be faithfully reproduced; yet that gripping tone quality, that variety of nuance, which experience in playing alone can give, are lacking. It is the same with one's reading. In school we study our Shakespeare and think we know him. I used to devour my Emerson and Browning — would go around with the books in my pocket. But I did not understand those writers then, though I thought I did. When we gain the wisdom of experience we see so much more in music, in art, in literature than we ever dreamed was there in our earlier days. So keep right on studying, exploring, gaining experience. Rightly directed, all experience should broaden and perfect our musical work, both of playing and teaching.

TABLE WORK

Years ago no one had ever heard of using the table as an ally of the keyboard, in piano teaching and practice. Nowadays the table is employed by many of the best teachers, to establish arm, hand and finger movements, to cultivate correct conditions of all playing members. The enlightened teacher knows this to be the clearest, quickest means of correcting bad touch and securing a good one. It is often necessary to take the mind off piano tone for awhile and pay special attention to condition, position and action; also to acquire precision and strength. If you cannot make correct movements at the table, you are not likely to make them at the keyboard. If you cannot move your fingers with precision away from the piano, how will you do so when you have keys to manipulate? For with keys you are thinking mainly of tones and tunes, and the attention is quite diverted from condition, position and action.

The best way to learn these things is away from the keyboard, away from sounds, till you are ready to make the right kind of sounds. The beginner should learn the simplest things — foundation principles of piano playing — at the table, quite undisturbed by tune or tempo. When condition and action are somewhat comprehended, it is time enough to begin work at the piano.

I speak from large experience when I urge every piano teacher who has not yet done so to look into this subject of table work. When you understand it you will find it most interesting and absorbing. Pupils also will be impressed and interested, *if* you can present it in such a way that they will see its value and what it will do for them. If you prove to them they will acquire foundational principles of finger action, touch, chord movements, accents, weight and so on, by working a short time away from the piano, you will doubtless find them quite willing to be guided by your judgment. Only you must know the subject thoroughly yourself.

TEACHING BACH

There is all the difference in the world in the way Bach's music is presented to a pupil. Here is one student's experience. She had gone to a new teacher who assigned her some Bach by writing the name of the book on a piece of paper and telling her to get it. The book was a collection of English Suites. The girl had not the slightest idea what these pieces meant, nor how to study them. She merely played the notes as though they were so many exercises and got nothing out of them.

She soon left that teacher and went to some one else. To him she said: "Whatever you do, don't give me Bach, for I hate him." He smiled and asked the reason; she told him. He gave her Bach, but handled the subject very differently from the first man. He explained the structure and meaning of the music, showing her how to study it. She soon, thanks to him, began to like it.

Another case was a young girl who had been allowed to play Bach in the most meaningless fashion. The girl said she found absolutely nothing in this music. I saw at once it had never been intelligently put before her. So I proceeded to open her eyes. I likened the piece we were considering to a story in literature, showing her where the subject was announced, the sentences and clauses of different kinds, and finally the conclusion. For the first time she saw there was a plan worked out in the music, that it really had a definite meaning. It was a revelation. Her face was illumined by these new ideas. She went home to study Bach with intelligent zeal.

Why cannot every teacher try the same plan? It is indeed a crime to hand out a volume of Bach, assign a Prelude or an Invention without a word of explanation. Then at the lesson hear the bewildered pupil stumble through her task, merely correcting false fingering, keys let up where they should be held down, and *vice versa*. Pupils seem to think they must play Bach just to learn the finicky fingering, or the arbitrary holding of this note or that. Of the meaning of the music, of the infinite variety of thought and feeling revealed in this wonderful music they often have not the faintest idea.

Let us change all this. Why should your pupil go on for another day thinking the grand old master Bach is stupid, dry and uninteresting, when you can so easily prevent such a misconception? Make your pupil acquainted with the Gavottes, Dances and lighter pieces of Bach, each explained, analyzed, thoroughly learned, memorized and played up to the required tempo. There are nine chances to one she will love them;

that instead of hating these pieces of Bach, she will be deeply interested in them and will be prepared to study the larger compositions later on, besides having the inestimable benefit of polyphonic training and thinking.

FOR THE BUSY TEACHER

Suppose the teacher has a large class of pupils, taking two and three lessons a week. She finds her only leisure is in the evening, which leaves her but little time for her own studies. Under these conditions it is difficult to concentrate on technic and pieces, yet she desires to keep up and not lose her facility.

I would say to her: If you are teaching young children, they probably have their lessons in the afternoon. How about the mornings? I have a number of pupil teachers who practice forenoons and teach the rest of the day. You can secure an hour or two in the mornings. If you have but an hour daily, give twenty minutes to technic. Arrange a schedule of the most important things, trills, scales, chords, arpeggios and octaves. Begin with a couple of stretching exercises, also gymnastic and pressure forms. Then add finger trills, scales and chords. Another day; gymnastics, trills, arpeggios and octaves. By careful planning you can go over fundamental forms in a week. With scales and arpeggios two majors and two minors, a day will soon go the rounds. As fingers become more fluent, "white key" scales may be played one day and "black keys" on another. The best of all this will be system, without which little worth while is accomplished.

HANDLING NEW PUPILS

How to handle the new pupil is a matter of vital importance to every serious teacher.

The new pupil who presents herself for lessons, is generally asked to play something; owing to timidity she does her worst perhaps. But the teacher of experience looks deeper than the outward appearance; he hopes to discover aptitude, talent, good foundation, understanding of fundamentals, good ear, good time sense and a well trained hand. How seldom any of these are found every teacher can bear witness.

Strange to say, though a pupil may be bright in other things and stand well in school studies, he is often far behind in musical intelligence.

Such a pupil was presented to me yesterday. She looked a bright young girl; said she had studied three years, producing her Bayer and Burgmuller. She could play absolutely nothing, no pieces, no scales, no technic, nothing. An attempt was made with one of the simple studies, but ended in dismal stumbling. You would have said this girl had never had a piano lesson in her life, yet she had spent three precious years wasting her time. Her only redeeming virtue was a good natural ear. She could name almost any key sounded in the center of the piano; she also had a good hand. These proved her teachers must have been hopelessly incompetent, otherwise she would have amounted to something.

Now, teachers, what would you do with such a pupil, how would you diagnose such a case? Here were hands entirely untrained, weak and all out of shape; no conception of what was needed on the technical side in order to play the piano. Would you appeal only to the musical sense in handling this pupil, and leave the performing sense still dormant and unawakened? I am aware there are people — perhaps many, more's the pity — who think musical sense is the paramount subject to bring before any pupil, while technical preparation is to be quite secondary, a something to be kept in the background.

According to my diagnose, this pupil had to lay a technical foundation before she could think of playing pieces which would give any pleasure to herself or her friends. She must learn to think, must be shown how to study intelligently. Our first lesson was spent principally at the table, learning to shape the hand, to move the fingers, to count, to exercise pressure and relaxation. If she can learn something of all these in one week, it is more than she has accomplished in three years.

In the second lesson we repeated the first exercises, adding arm movements for chords, accent, pressure, ear training, drill in sight reading and so on.

How many teachers would follow my plan of

going to the bottom and building up a foundation, or how many would take the easier (?) and pleasanter (?) path of studies and pieces? You will probably tell me that in order to interest the girl and have something to show for the labor, you must give pieces. I can say to you that after six months this girl could play quarters, eighth triplet and sixteenth notes to the metronome beat with ease; she knew triads of every key; had done trills, scales, arpeggios and octaves, several studies, and had half a dozen pieces memorized. She had not been turned against music, as so many teachers fear will be the case if thorough technic is taught. On the contrary, she remarked, in her quaint way: "I like my piano study; music interests me very much." And this girl only practiced one hour a day!

IS LOVE OF MUSIC IMPAIRED BY CORRECT SCHOOLING IN MUSIC?

Quite in line with what we have just considered, is the following letter, just received from a teacher.

" I have lately read an article in one of the musical journals, entitled: 'Musical and Unmusical Education,' in which the writer seems to think music should not be taught along educational lines; 'that music has lost its spirit and purpose by reason of endeavoring to utilize the principles and practices of regular school studies in the study of music.' For years I have felt that music *should* be taught along educational lines, with the same thoroughness that mathematics or any school study is taught. My experience bears out this belief. I shall be glad to have your opinion in the matter, for I have seen that you look at things in a sensible light."

I wrote back that she was quite right in her surmise of my sentiments; that I do stand unreservedly for thorough piano teaching; that I believed in teaching music as thoroughly as any school study. Until it is so taught, we shall continue to have slipshod work and quantities of poor players and teachers. Pupils who only think of music as an ear tickling diversion, can be gathered by scores any day. They amount to nothing; they only have a bare smattering of notes, with no foundation and no understanding. They are a trial to themselves and to everybody who hears them. No wonder they don't care much for music.

Let us look squarely at this fetich of getting pleasure out of playing the piano without any labor. Does this kind of smattering really give any pleasure in the end? Suppose the student has only the pleasant, entertaining, easy side put before him. Suppose the senses are cultivated and the intellectual or technical side is kept in the background. It is then all feeling and emotion, with nothing to balance it on the educational side. How will such a pupil express himself? He may love music and would like to make himself understood, but cannot, because he has no real knowledge; only the senses and emotions have been appealed to; mental training has been quite secondary. Such a pupil will probably bemoan his fate a little later, and then he will blame those who taught him the wrong end first. With his love for music he has no ability to execute it. Will it deaden his love for music to know how it is put together, its key and time signatures, the analysis of its chords and harmonies? No, for he can then use his mind, his intelligence.

A young lady came to me the other day for lessons. She was playing Liszt's 2nd Rhapsodie. I suggested a little piece of Bach, which happened to be in the key of G minor. I asked her the signature; she had no idea. I asked for other signatures; she seemed equally ignorant. I mentally set down her former teachers as equally ignorant. Would this girl's regard for music be lessened had she been able to tell key signatures and chord and scale formations? Not a bit of it. In these days we are working for more and more intelligence, not less and less. We want to teach music wisely, interestingly and at the same time as thoroughly as any school lesson is taught. We will not fear to require the pupil to use his mind, his mental qualities. We know that "Mind is Everything." The sooner we realize this in music teaching, the better work we will do, the more we will interest our pupils and the greater progress they will make.

THE CITY VERSUS THE COUNTRY TEACHER

The teacher of music in a large city has little idea of the varied labors of her sister in the small town. The latter cannot follow one branch of teaching exclusively, she must combine several. Her preference may lie either for piano or voice, but she must be prepared to teach both in her vicinity. Not only these, but she must sometimes take pupils on the violin, and often on the organ, besides having charge of the church choir. We have been told often enough that a Jack of all trades is master of none; that this is a day of specializing, and that students wish to specialize in each line. Yet there are many teachers in small towns who are expected to take pupils on at least two instruments besides the voice. How shall they be encouraged to keep abreast of the times?

One such teacher came to the metropolis to get "freshened up," as she said. She longed to find inspiration, new ideas, up-to-date methods. She was hungry for music and the artistic performance of it. For to her little town no artist ever came; no great playing or singing was to be heard, from one end of the year to the other.

This teacher did a wise thing in dropping her work for three or four weeks right in the heart of the season, and coming to the music center to study, hear music and gain a new impetus. She took a course of lessons from specialists in the three branches she was teaching, piano, violin and voice. "I do not care particularly to work on pieces; what I am after is principles," she said. "It suits me just as well to discuss the subjects, as to play myself. I want ideas. I also want to hear music, for I am starving for it."

Let us turn for a moment to the other side of the picture. The well established specialist in the large city is the one to whom the country teacher will apply for help and incentive. He must be ready to give it. He must have the principles to give, in clear and condensed form. He must have a remedy for every such case. As a musical pedagogue remarked: "There can be no patent on musical discoveries; we must be willing to give out what we have learned or discovered for ourselves, in order to help others." If we are conscious we have the knowledge which will benefit others, how can we hold it back; how can we make a secret of it? Rather let us do all we can to help the struggling teacher who has found her vocation in a small town, for her duties are heavy and her opportunities are few.

CHAPTER II

LAYING THE FOUNDATION

HOW ONE MUSICAL EDUCATOR BEGINS

THE Professor * stood before his class, serious, alert, vigorous, in spite of his advanced years. Under shaggy brows his glance was penetrating but kindly. A white, close cropped beard gave him a venerable aspect. His flexible hands were held in front of him, the fingertips touching — a little way he had. A lifetime of struggle to inculcate true principles of piano playing lay behind him, and yet he was as eager to carry on the warfare as ever.

Before him sat a class of teachers, pianists, and advanced students, all of whom had taught and played the piano for years. They had come from various parts of the country, because they wanted to learn more of the art of teaching or of handling their instrument. Some had technical defects of long standing, others wanted new and more thorough methods. All had a teachable spirit, or they would not have been there. They believed this veteran in the field could help them solve their problems and answer their various questions.

"How many people play the piano?" began the Professor: "I will answer, thousands of

* A. K. Virgil.

them. The world is full of smatterers, of those who have fooled with the piano for years. How many do you know who play the piano well, or even fairly well? Very few; so few you can almost count them on the fingers of one hand. Why are there so many playing the piano badly? Because, from the very start, they have been trying to do things they were not prepared to do."

"My heavens, that's so!" exclaimed one of the men before him, almost starting from his seat.

"Yes," repeated the Professor, "people are always trying to do what they can't do. Now I say to my pupils —'I shall never ask you to do anything you are not able to perform. Every step will be so thoroughly explained and shown that it will be perfectly easy. We will go from step to step in logical order. If, as we take them, you tell me each step is easy, I shall expect you to do them all perfectly. Piano playing is easy, if you go at it the right way, though many people make mighty hard work of it, and then never get anywhere into the bargain. I remember meeting De Pachman the morning after he had played a long and difficult program. The little man was wrathy. 'Here is one fool critic,' he burst out, 'who talks about one of the works I gave *with such smoothness and perfection, in spite of its stupendous difficulties.* Of course it was easy for me. If it hadn't been easy I would not have played it!' And so I say to you; make piano playing easy from the start.

"As my students sit before a table for their

first lesson, I say to them: 'I am your friend
and I am sure you are mine. I am here to help
you, but I expect you to promise to do just as
I tell you. You are friends with each other.
If you really want to help your neighbors, and
you notice any point in which you can help them
it will be a kindness to do so.

"Students are generally afflicted with twin
vices, ignorance and laziness. We want to replace these vices with the twin virtues, Intelligence and Perseverance; with these we will conquer.

"Before seating themselves at the table, I re-
quest my beginning class to stand and acquire
an easy, flexible condition of body. If you allow the weight to rest on the heel of your foot,
you institute stiffness at once. Throw the body-
weight on the ball of the foot and you at once
relax. You can then turn the body from side to
side, which will cause the arms to swing naturally from the shoulder, *if* they first hang loosely.
Thus an idea of Condition is at once implanted
in the mind of my student.

"At the table we consider, first of all, the mental side of piano playing. I show them it is the
mind that controls all movements; if they mentally understand an exercise they can easily do
it.

"On slips of paper they write down three
maxims, namely: 'Mind is Everything,' 'Concentration alone Conquers,' 'Knowledge is
Power.' I then ask them to close their eyes and

not to open them till I give permission. If you haven't enough control to keep your eyelids shut, you have not enough to play a piece on the piano. After speaking a bit, I ask those who think they can recite those maxims, to raise their hands. As each sentence is recited, I ask how many words it contains? Three. How many words all together? Nine. I want to say those nine words will do more for you in mental training than any other nine words in the language. If Mind is Everything — and it is — you must use it to get your lesson with. Concentration will conquer every part of the lesson, and, as Knowledge is Power, you will come to your next lesson, prepared fully and consciously to recite and play all I have given you, without a mistake.

"Our next move is to study position. Hand position is a very important item. You may have all the *soul* in the world, but if you have a bad position of hand, arm and fingers, you will fail to express it. There is just one right way for you to hold your hand, and shape your fingers; that is the truth. We are here to study Truth, and nothing less will satisfy us. When I see a hand correctly shaped, it looks beautiful to me, for there is nothing so beautiful as Truth!

"Following hand shaping comes finger action. I will show you on my hand; just look here. I will make three movements with the index finger. The first shall be slow and steady, an almost imperceptible motion; this is for control. The second is an easy swing, for suppleness. The

third is a quick start, for exactness. This is a
playing movement, one we always use at the keyboard.

"There are four fundamental principles which
underlie piano playing. They are: Condition,
Position, Action and Order. We have considered three. The fourth, Order, means going
straight through the exercise without a mistake.
These four principles lie at the foundation of
playing, just as the four principles of numbers
— addition, subtraction, multiplication and di-
vision — lie at the foundation of mathematics.
You don't multiply when you should divide, nor
add when you ought to subtract. If you do, you
don't get the right answer. So it is in music
study. We learn to apply the right principle,
the correct movement, to the exercise, and we get
the right answer — we can do the technical problem as it should be done. If I had not been perfectly certain there were laws governing piano
technic, I would not have sought them. Now I
am convinced of their truth. I do not claim to
have discovered these principles, for they have
always existed. But I may have pointed to ways
of working them out, as well as to the necessity
of understanding them. As for myself, I have
studied them from the living model; in fact, from
the great exponents of piano playing, from Rubinstein down. I studied the performance of
eighteen great pianists and talked with them on
these themes. In doing so I made an unexpected
discovery; that they themselves did not know

how they produced the various effects we marveled at. If they had known, they could have produced those effects at will; but as they did not know exactly, it was often guess work. Rubinstein played the most beautiful, sonorous chords that could be imagined, with combined wrist and arm movements. All he could say about his manner of doing them was, that if one played chords with stiff wrists, one would produce hard tones. Paderewski played marvelous scales, yet could not explain just how he did them. If he could have done this, every player would have hastened to obey, for the playing of the great Pole was the wonder of his time. I often discussed technical problems with him. On one occasion he wanted me to take hold of a pupil of his and teach him to play good scales. The boy was bright and intelligent, and I taught him for about a month. Then Paderewski returned to the city and sent for us to come to him. He at once requested the young man to sit down at the piano and play some scales. By this time the student had learned how to perform an excellent scale, for he had learned the principles underlying scale playing. The master was highly pleased with the result, yet almost angry at the same instant. 'Why didn't you play such a scale before?' he demanded. The answer nonplussed him. 'Because you never showed me how!' Then the Polish pianist pushed the lad aside, sat down and played scales after his own marvelous fashion. Of course he could play a

perfect scale; had he not devoted much time and
hard labor to that particular thing for years?
Add labor and genius and the product will be
perfection. But he could not explain just *how*
it was done, neither could others, famous in the
pianistic field, whom I consulted.

"Another thing you must bear in mind. The
gifted artist, through perseverance, has arrived
— though by knowing the principles he could
have greatly shortened his journey. But it is
for the moderately endowed I am working; for
those who, if their efforts are rightly directed,
can become excellent players and efficient
teachers, capable of doing great good in the
world. Without this knowledge they would only
flounder about and never amount to anything.
All cannot be geniuses, but any one who studies
the piano in the right way can do accurate, mu-
sicianly work. It is not only knowing the principles of piano playing, but it is in applying them
that mental power and understanding come in.
Thus I repeat, with the right use of the mind,
piano playing becomes easy and natural, and we
are able to express our inner feelings and emotions through it."

It would be pleasant to follow the Professor
through subsequent lessons to his class. Of one
thing we can be very sure; that for every lesson,
from first to last, and all the time, he is just as
careful, painstaking and thorough as it is possible for a mortal to be. No one can slide
through and do slipshod work, and escape detec-

tion. The good Professor is ever on the alert,
ever carrying the highest ideal before the student, urging him onward and upward.

IS A THOROUGH FOUNDATION NECESSARY?

Many teachers are trying to instruct their
pupils in music, with little or no thought to the
sub-structure they are building upon, as though
a thorough foundation were not necessary. In
fact they seem to avoid this all important subject, even leaving it out altogether.

A case of this sort came to me not long ago.
The lady had a great natural love for music and
the ambition to study. She had not been able
to take up music as a child; as a young woman
she had decided to begin. She was anxious to
make up for lost time.

Here was surely an opportunity for a serious
teacher to lay a good foundation, for the pupil
was willing and eager to work. But alas, the
teacher she had chosen was not equal to the task:
she gave the ordinary exercises, then pieces
which were much too difficult.

After a few months the scene changed. A
professor took charge of the instruction of this
adult beginner. He, too, failed to lay a foundation. His prescription was the Philipp Technics, an interesting work in its way, but far
beyond the comprehension of this beginner. He
also prescribed a Mozart Fantaisie and some
Beethoven, but the pupil was entirely unprepared

for them.   She had not had one principle clearly
presented to her, nor could she move fingers or
arms, as she had absolutely no command of
either.

What was the result?   After a year of hopeless floundering, the lady was quite discouraged,
though her love for music and her desire to play
were as strong as ever, but she felt she had not
found the right path.

She has now begun at the real beginning.   She
is now learning principles of touch, technic,
rhythm and tone production.   Each week marks
improvement in understanding and achieve-
ment.   She feels she has made a correct start,
and nothing can hinder her progress in the right
direction.

Meeting her first teacher, she asked:

"Why did you not give me a real foundation
at the beginning, when you started me?   That
was the thing I most needed."

"Because I was afraid you would think it
too dry; I feared you would not stand for it."

When will teachers of the piano learn that
honesty is the best policy?   When will they
stand up boldly for thorough foundational instruction?   And if they are not prepared to lay
a good foundation for the pupil, why not study
modern methods until they become competent
to do thorough honest work?   Why not put their
mind to this absorbing topic of foundation building, and master it?

THE PRACTICAL SIDE OF A THOROUGH
FOUNDATION

A talented child of nine was brought to me to be looked over and "polished up." She had been offered an engagement to do some public playing, but was obliged to play at least half a dozen pieces perfectly before the contract could be signed.

The teacher of this child had tried to make her a show pupil without giving sufficient attention to the foundation. She was playing such pieces as the Rachmaninoff Prelude in C sharp minor and Liszt's Love Dream, No. 3, both beyond her from a technical viewpoint, as well as because of her small hands. She could read quickly, but as little was required of her on the technical side, and she was not taught to analyze the music, her practice consisted in simply playing the pieces over and over, until it became very monotonous.

The child was shown the difference between playing for friends in the home circle and going out before an audience. It is true her playing gave pleasure in the home, but would not pass muster in public. What was the trouble?

The trouble was that the foundation she had originally received was allowed to lapse with the last teacher, until it was almost destroyed. Fingers had been permitted to lie flat upon the keys until they had become more or less inert and lifeless; chords were unprepared and slovenly, while phrasing was quite ignored.

A corrective was administered at once. Fingers had to be curved and made firm and the hand brought into position. Finger action had to be established, and a clean, clear tone production insisted upon. Meanwhile the pieces had to be analyzed in detail, mistakes in rhythm and phrasing corrected and the various touches applied.

All these troubles and delays could have been avoided if the foundational training had been carried on systematically and logically.

The right way — the practical way is to start aright and build on a sure foundation. But it is not practical to lose sight of that careful beginning and allow faults to undermine the foundation of the building. There is always a technical foundation to be built. After that a foundation of slow, careful, thorough analytical study for every piece that is taken up. Therefore look to the foundation!

ARTISTIC MOVEMENTS IN PIANO PLAYING

The sort of movements necessary to produce a good tone on the piano, or the fact that there are certain movements that are necessary for tone production, is a subject which few students, or teachers even, consider. If you speak of movements they look at you in astonishment. What movements? They have never heard movement emphasized as necessary to produce effects. They have never learned that, in order to play chords with sonorous, ringing tone, a rotary movement of arms and wrists is required. Slow, sustained chords may also be produced by the down movement of the arm, while for stac- cato chords the hands spring up from the key- board, assisted in their upward sweep by an impulse from the body.

This so-called rotary movement can be applied to individual fingers as well as to chords. The rotary arm movement applies to every instance where a rich, mellow tone is desired. The move- ment itself is very graceful; the arm and wrist are relaxed and the weight thus gained descends to the finger tips. If the passage is slow and stately, a very dramatic effect can be produced by this easy weighted condition of hands and arms.

As has been said, few students seem to be acquainted with these plastic movements, for teachers in general do not teach them. Even many well-known pianists before the public to- day do not sufficiently employ them. Yet they are not difficult to learn and at once begin to impart ease, grace, freedom of action and variety to the tone. Those who study with the writer always use them; indeed these principles are among the first which are taught to students, as they correct and eliminate awkward stiffness, giving freedom and poise. This is a subject which piano teachers should look into; especially are students advised to consider it. They should take thought of the appearance and movement in their playing; whether it has the ease and freedom it ought to have; also whether the tone has sufficient power and resonance. If the playing is lacking in these respects, look to the movements you are making — and teaching. They are doubtless at fault. Correct them and the playing will improve in tone quality and effect.

CHAPTER III

POINTS ON TECHNICAL TRAINING

SLOW VERSUS QUICK FINGER MOVEMENTS

I AM frequently asked whether pupils in the early stages should use slow or quick finger action. My answer to all such inquiries has ever been in favor of easy, quick, exact finger movements. My reasons are as follows.

Precision must be established from the start. This precision can only be accomplished when the fingers make decided movements. Precision can never be gained by slow, uncertain action.

Clearness. Great teachers insist on clearness of touch in piano playing. This distinctness is required in every branch of art. It is a necessity for the orator, the singer, the violinist, the 'cellist, as well as for the pianist. Listen to a great violin player and you will notice how every tone, even in the most rapid, whispered passages, stands out clear and distinct from the others. In order to acquire this clearness on the piano, we must make quick, exact movements; slow, lazy ones will blur everything.

Rhythm. In order to create exactness of rhythm, you must make exact finger movements. If the action is slow and indolent, there is apt to be much indecision in the rhythm. Precision of rhythm is one of the first and most necessary requirements.

I would like to recall a bit of personal experience by way of illustration. At one period of my musical studies, I was placed with a foremost American pianist and teacher. This man was a concert artist of wide reputation. His method of teaching, however, was quite different from anything I had hitherto discovered. Instead of the quick, alert movements and firm touch I had striven so assiduously to cultivate, he advocated slow movements and soft touch. This method may be beneficial if taken in small doses, but soft, slow movements, practiced continuously for six months, will certainly take all force, exactness and vim out of one's playing; they did out of mine. It took a long time to recover from this regimen and regain my equilibrium.

Insist on easy, quick and springy finger movements in your pupils. Clearness is a first principle. Establish clearness, exactness and precision at the very beginning; your pupils will be grateful to you later on.

A QUESTION OF STIFFNESS

A common fault with all sorts of players is a stiff wrist. Rigid wrists are patent to even a casual observer. It is a fault easily recognized by both eye and ear. For a stiff wrist is usually elevated and out of shape. The tone produced by this position and condition is generally hard and dry.

While wrist stiffness is easy to detect, there is a stiffness of arm which is not so often thought of. Yet to play with good tone and effect, we need absolute freedom of arm. If this seems a new idea to some, it is because they have not considered the important and vital rôle played by the arm in piano technic and performance. One has but to watch the arm movement and control exercised by a great artist, to be convinced that the arm is to be held entirely pliable, so that unrestricted arm-weight may be brought to the finger tips. The pianist's arm moves up and down the keyboard with the poise and security of a bird in flight. Graceful, easy movements of arms carry the hands wherever they are needed. So the artist uses them.

But the amateur often has quite another understanding of the use of the arm. He is stiff and constrained, with very little freedom of movement. Why does he not gain the freedom and poise which the artist deems so essential? It is not difficult to acquire these conditions. Proper technical material, practiced with intelligent understanding of the principles involved, will give him these essentials. Therefore, if the player wishes to gain freedom and control of arm, study the swinging arm movements and control will soon be won.

WEAK THUMBS

A young teacher writes of the difficulty she encounters in pupils having weak thumbs. She complains thumb joints are so weak and wobbly as to be almost double-jointed.

I can truly sympathize with this difficulty, for I have found it in students of all kinds and conditions. One young woman, who had studied with various excellent teachers, was the most serious case of this trouble I have ever had to handle. Her former masters had given up in despair; the thumb still remained weak and crooked. I applied vigorous measures and at last succeeded in effecting a cure.

With small pupils the matter is much simpler, for they have not played so long in the wrong way, and they like to hold their hands in a pretty position and make them look well. I use various gymnastic exercises, pulling out the thumb, working the muscles between it and the hand. I then place the hand on table or keys, in correct position, and require the thumb to give a number of accent impulses, not strong enough, however, to put the hand out of position. Each day the pressure can be made a little stronger. This treatment of combined massage and pressure, with constant care and watching, will at last render the finger shapely and strong. If other fingers are weak and bending, the only efficient remedy is to stop everything and get right down to business of correcting faults of hand and fingers.

OVERCOMING STIFFNESS

Stiffness can always be traced to a mental source. If you can once realize the difference of sensation in your hand and arm by the condition of looseness and stiffness, you can induce one or the other at will. You can soon learn to relax by raising the arm, then letting it drop at your side, a dead weight; you know it is then relaxed. Form the hand in playing position on a table and raise and lower the wrist. The wrist must of necessity be loose to make this movement. Now exercise the finger, at the same time preserving the same feeling of rest in the wrist. With care, thought and slow practice, all stiffness should soon disappear. It is not an easy thing, at first, to keep the wrist loose while seeking to acquire firmness of finger; but this must be done.

EXCESSIVE RELAXATION

A teacher writes:

"We hear so much about relaxation these days. But is there not danger in overdoing the principle? I had not realized this danger until last evening, when I happened to listen to a certain pianist. His playing seemed to me singularly ineffective, and I sought the cause. I first noticed hand position; the knuckles were much sunken and wobbled up and down. The wrists kept moving up and down too. With all this looseness there was nothing firm, no real arm-weight, and the tone was thin and uncertain. Was this the result of the wobbling sunken knuckles? This player is a teacher, but it seems to me if he teaches these ideas, he will be doing more harm than good."

You are quite right; there is great danger in over relaxation. The principle can be so over-done that it can even do more harm than good, in the hands of those who do not understand. I am reminded of a conversation with Mme. Carreno, in which she said: "The secret of power lies in relaxation, or, I might say, power *is* relaxation. This word is very apt to be mis-understood. You tell pupils to relax, and if they do not understand when and how, they get no-where. Relaxation does not mean to flop all over the piano; it means, rather, to loosen just where it is needed and nowhere else. I came into my studio one morning," she continued, "and found some of the pupils rolling and flop-ping all over the piano, and enquired what was the matter with them. 'Oh, we are trying to relax!' So I showed them again where and why they were all wrong, and what the right way was."

Thus one can do great damage with false ideas about relaxation. If you watch the greatest pianists you will find they have firm knuckles, and hold their hands in an arched position. They never allow knuckle joints to fall in. It does not look well in the first place, and in the second, shows much weakness in the hand. I believe this principle is sadly misunderstood among the rank and file of teachers and students of the piano. It is high time they should see the light, learn these things correctly and know how to teach them. It is really not at all difficult to form the hand in an arched position at the same time holding the wrist loose. Neither of these points is beyond the comprehension of the average beginner; further progress depends on their application. They are the foundation stones upon which the superstructure of technic must be built. Why do not teachers of the piano insist on these fundamentals? Those who do, accomplish much in the right direction.

THE QUESTION OF RELAXED WEIGHT

We were studying Mozart's Fantaisie in D minor, my little pupil and I. So much depends on clean-cut articulation, phrasing and punctuation, to make the interpretation of this piece effective and artistic. There are any number of places where groups of three notes occur, each one of the three to be played in a different way. The first note short, the second legato, the third released with up-wrist movement. My little pupil could not seem to apply the principle of relaxed arm weight to the first and second keys; she could not drop down on the middle key of the group with the right condition. I caught her sleeve, lifting her arm and hand; they were light.

I let go; the arm remained in the air, showing it was not relaxed, otherwise it would have instantly fallen to the lap. The pupil had made good chord and other movements in playing; but had not sensed the all important idea of Condition, without which relaxed weight and its application are not possible.

No doubt many teachers find difficulty in making this principle clear to pupils. It takes some time before relaxation becomes second nature — before it is so thoroughly understood that it can be employed instantly and constantly. The teacher must be ever on the alert for condition, watching to see it is being rightly used, that the pupil grasps the meaning and need of relaxation, also when and where to relax.

WEAK FINGER-JOINTS

A young player writes:

" I am troubled about a certain condition of my hand, and that is the weakness of the nail-joints of my fingers. If I try to play with any power, these joints cave in and are very unsteady. I have played the piano for a number of years without ever noticing this condition, as my early teachers never said anything about it. As I read and learn more about hand position and condition, I gradually realize the weakness of my fingers, and have located the trouble at the nail-joint. Lately I spoke to the professor I am working with about this fault, and asked what I should do to remedy it. He had never even noticed it. To my surprise, he made quite light of the whole thing, saying musicians no longer bothered themselves about making the nail-joint firm. He even went so far as to say one could get a more beautiful tone with bending fingers. Will you give me some advice?"

That you have discovered the weakness of your fingers shows you are awake and thinking along the right lines. It *is* of the highest importance to cultivate firmness in the shaping joints of the fingers, no matter what your present teacher may say to the contrary. Leschetizky, one of the greatest teachers of the piano, required rock-like firmness of the nail-joint, and he formed some of the greatest pianists of our time. He insisted strongly on this point; it was one of the few absolute principles he laid down. For, while he disclaimed having a cut-and-dried method, he averred his so-called method consisted of loose wrists and arms, arched hand and firm knuckles.

The beginner, rightly taught, learns at once to arch the hand, to cultivate freedom and elasticity of knuckle-joints and firmness of finger joints. Much of this can be taught at a table. He begins at the table to try the strength of his fingers by putting a gentle pressure on them : pressure is increased as the fingers grow stronger, learn to resist the weight and " stand up " under it.

If you wish to overcome this weakness in your hand, why not put yourself through a drill, dropping difficult pieces for a short time, until the hand is in better condition to master them.

You may discover other faults and weaknesses at the same time, which need to be eliminated.

It is very beneficial to have a renovating period for one's technic, to overhaul the playing mechanism. The owner of a fine piece of machinery keeps it well oiled and in perfect repair. Just so the pianist must see that his technical machine is kept in perfect condition, that it may give the best service.

AN OUTWARD SIGN OF RELAXATION

Some one asks:

"How shall I know I am relaxed when I play the piano? I think I am relaxed, especially when I play chords, but I am not sure. How can I really tell?"

Relaxation is a condition. Relaxation comprises relaxed weight of arm on the finger tips, and thus on the keys. This loose sensation, with a feeling of heaviness in the arm, must be coupled with a certain staying quality to prevent the hand and fingers from going "all to pieces"—from falling all in a heap, as it were. Fruit juice, prepared for jelly, must be cooked enough to enable it to *stand*, otherwise it will be too soft and run. This homely illustration is to the point. Just so the hand; it must have stability enough to keep its position, although the muscles of wrist and arm are relaxed. Just as the jelly is not stiff and hard, but pliable; it will give and yield. But still it is *set* and will not go to pieces.

As for the sign of relaxation, that is to be found in the movement. If you come down *straight* on the keys of the chord, and lift your hand *straight* up again, you have the movement of rigidity, and your tone will be hard and dry, because you have used the movement of stiffness, and some of your joints are stiff where they should be pliable and yielding. You must replace this stiff movement with the opposite condition — with a movement which indicates pliable weight. This is a sort of rotary movement of arm, which combines the hinges of wrist, elbow and shoulder. When you lift up your arm from the chord or single key, you should start the wrist first, and this act draws the finger up with it. This slight rolling movement, with relaxed arms and loose wrists will give you the outward and visible sign of the condition of relaxation. If you do not make this movement you are probably not relaxed; that is to say you do not give the tone the benefit of this relaxed swing of the arm. It is this relaxed swing of the arm which gives the chord or note its power and resonance.

LEFT HAND STUDY

A teacher asks:

"What shall I do for a pupil who has injured, temporarily, her right hand? She is quite upset and thinks she must stop all lessons and practice. Is there any way I can aid her?"

This question is liable to come up in any

teacher's experience, and the resourceful teacher must be ready to handle it.

Has it not occurred to you to advise some left hand work for the pupil with disabled right hand? The left hand is often more unruly than the right, anyhow. Your pupil may really need some left hand work, which will now bring it up to a more efficient condition.

The left hand can now practice all sorts of technic; in fact, everything that has been done with two hands may be done singly. Thumb and finger training, trills, octaves, chords and scales may be brought up to greater perfection. If the student be advanced, portions of pieces having difficult left hand passages, for instance the octaves in Chopin's Polonaise, Op. 53, may be studied.

Then there are various pieces written for left hand alone. A simple one is the pretty Solfeggietto, of Emmanuel Bach, turned into a one-hand study by A. R. Parsons. An interesting Nocturne by Scriabine is a good concert number and an interesting piece to have in one's repertoire. A fine Left Hand Suite, by Rheinberger, contains three parts, each ingeniously built up, interesting and melodious.

Thus you see there is no real reason for the pupil to feel obliged to stop lessons and practice for the cause you mention. It is well for parents to understand this side of the question. Temporary disablement of five fingers need not interrupt musical instruction; for a capable teacher can continue to impart necessary knowledge, and can give the other hand plenty to do.

It is the same — in the early stages — with the required amount of practice. Pupils often want to omit lessons because they have lost some practice hours during the week. This is no reason for remaining away from the lesson which has been arranged for long in advance. The teacher will be doubtless glad to take up some point which, for lack of time, has had to be crowded out. The student can always profit by an hour of instruction in an art in which there is so much to learn!

THE WRONG END OF RELAXATION

The artist-teacher says to the anxious student: "You don't relax — your wrists are stiff; just let go and relax."

"But how?" queries the anxious one. "I would gladly do it if I knew just how."

"How? Do it just as you see me do. See, I do it *so;* I am not stiff."

The pupil tries to imitate and departs, thinking he has the right idea. But he may be very far from the truth. Not gaining anything definite from the artist, he proceeds to acquire the desired looseness and relaxation as best he may. The result often is that he relaxes "all over," that is his hand, arm and fingers flop about, with no staying power or quality anywhere. He is indeed relaxing with a vengeance. But never mind; he is happy because he fancies he is on the right road, when the truth is he has begun at the wrong end.

The pianist should not relax "all over," but only in the place where it is necessary. The places where relaxation is necessary are at wrist, arm and shoulder, not at the finger joints or knuckles.

I had two cases of this mistaken relaxation come to me recently. Both players had studied with well known artists. Both had been told to relax, but had never been shown how to do it, or what movements and exercises should be used to secure this condition. The result was they merely "flopped," and called it by the magic name of relaxation.

After some stability has been established in the hand and fingers, it is a simple thing to acquire relaxation, weight and poise in the arms. But don't begin on your arms — though you may do a few gymnastics with them — until you have some idea of how to hold your hand and move your fingers. Establish right conditions in hand and fingers; then they can stand up under relaxed weight of arms, brought to bear on them. Without this preparation it will be the same old "flop" again, which leads nowhere, and results only in mussy, ineffective playing.

THE GLISSANDO

A young player and teacher asks:

"I have a lot of trouble with glissando runs. Whenever I try to do them I have to desist almost immediately, because of the pain. If I continue the finger soon bleeds. There must be some way of doing them without bruising one's digits. Can you explain how this is to be accomplished?"

There is a certain knack in executing the glissando. It is found in the principle of gliding easily over the keys with one finger, but not "digging in" while doing this. If the student can avoid this one thing, he can soon learn to draw the finger lightly along the keys without effort or injury.

Begin with the third finger, right hand, low position, with hand turning outward, until it is nearly parallel with the keys. Allow the third joint of finger to be so flexible that it will vibrate as it passes over each key. Then move the hand light and quickly up the keyboard. If the hand is held in this position and maintains this condition, a smooth, flowing glissando may result. If more power is required, elevate the hand somewhat. The thumb may also be used, with the third joint flexible.

CHAPTER IV

THE STUDY OF RHYTHM

THE LACK OF RHYTHM SENSE

MANY teachers do not realize how deficient their pupils are in rhythmic sense. Pupils can be tested by requiring them to beat time to a simple passage having a few varieties of note values. They may have a general idea of the different kinds of " time," but are often incapable of being exact as to count or beat. As soon as they are asked to count aloud or play with the metronome, they are quite lost, " put out " by the remorseless beat.

The teacher who would be successful must realize this inherent weakness, and make her work especially strong and clear on this point. Various means may be used to establish the feeling for rhythm. One is tapping with the end of a lead pencil on the table, to match the beat of the metronome. Easier, because more a part of the learner's very self, is the tapping with foot in time with the metronome. Simple rhythms may be followed by more complex forms, until the student is able to beat out a whole sonata movement. All this does not come in a moment; it is a gradual growth. But it should be begun

119

with the earliest lessons and carried on and up systematically.

PLAYING IN TIME

A teacher writes:

"I have a pupil who seems to have great trouble with time. He can play and read quite difficult pieces, but stumbles and does not keep correct time in them. He has a metronome and sets it going, believing by that act to remedy the evil."

Your pupil probably has two particular faults: he practices too fast and does not count aloud. He must at once stop fast, careless practice — which is the root of all evil — and learn to work slowly. At the same time he must learn to Count Aloud! there is no help for it, it must be done. He must hear the beat, be conscious of it, and not rest till his count agrees with his metronome. Of what use is it to set the metronome going and never keep with it. He must study simpler music, until these faults are conquered.

A METRONOME IN YOUR HEAD

"Have you a metronome in your head?" I asked a little music student. One teacher said recently: "I have drilled my pupils so constantly in rhythmic exercises, always using the metronome, that I feel I really have one in my head."

The only way to have a metronome in one's

head, that is, to have a thoroughly grounded sense of rhythm, is to make good use of this valuable little monitor. Let us stand up for this tireless little "policeman," as such a great authority as Josef Hofmann calls it. When I hear of teachers, and schools also, going against the metronome — and I frequently hear of such cases — I know where to place them. They are far behind the times, back numbers. How can they talk of progressive study, when they are in such an old-fashioned rut? They are holding to the old-time view that music is only an amusement, with which one need not be exact. They do not seem to know that rhythm is the life of music. Even talented people need a lot of drill before exact rhythm becomes second nature, so inground as to be unassailable. Then think of the people who are not talented, who flounder helplessly with note values, without knowing what is the trouble. The trouble is Lack of Rhythmic Sense. The Remedy is: have a metronome in your head. Will you use the remedy and be cured?

BEATING TIME WITH THE FOOT

A teacher is troubled by a habit of beating time with the foot, and wants to know how she can break herself of it.

In regard to time beating with the foot, you may be surprised to learn that some very good artists consider this process an excellent way to acquire an innate sense of rhythm. I can men-

tion a pianist, Mr. Thuel Burnham, who believes
tapping with the foot inculcates an inner feeling
for rhythm, since it must come from the player
himself, it is within him, rather than from outside. Of course the tapping belongs to the hours
of study and must be ignored when one plays for
others or before the public. If you cannot dispense with it then, you will have to take yourself well in hand, to see that you curb this action
in public. No one can do this for you; it is a
mental act, to be performed by mind.

NECESSITY OF COUNTING, AND COUNTING ALOUD

Not long ago we wrote ungently on the necessity of counting aloud, and find that it helped
various teachers. One writes: "A pupil of
mine was very averse to counting, and of course
failed in Accuracy. I had labored long on this
one thing, but my instruction was not sufficiently
heeded. When I found the article in the Round
Table, I showed it to the pupil, remarking:
'You see I am not alone in requiring you to
count aloud when you practice. Here is one of
our greatest authorities requiring the same
thing.' She saw the point, and has given me
little or no trouble since."

We will urge this point again with all teachers
who have to do with young pupils in whatever
grade. It is of the greatest importance to establish the counting-aloud-habit, from the very
first. This one thing will do more than any
other one thing to make the pupil accurate and

attentive. We have seen its good results over and over again. We also see the evil results of neglecting this basic principle. Many careless, indifferent teachers do not insist on the counting principle, and one cannot wonder they turn out slovenly, indifferent pupils.

Another thing. Those slovenly, indifferent habits, once formed, are almost impossible to get rid of. Various cases come to mind. One of a young man, an ambitious, eager worker, who, in spite of all the time and labor spent on difficult pieces, usually " falls down " as to count and rhythm each week, when he comes to his lesson. Though he practices with the best of intentions, the habit of neglect is so fixed he does not seem able to break it. The lessons are apt to be a trial to both teacher and student, mainly for this reason. Be strict in this matter of Counting Aloud. Strictness now will call down blessings on your head later on.

THE COUNT AGAIN

" I can't count this piece and scarcely dare go to my next lesson with it; can you help me? "

This wail of discouragement came from the pupil of one of the popular pianist-teachers.

" Show me your piece and tell me what the trouble is," I said.

" It's the Grieg Nocturne, and, as you see, has two notes against three. I have never in my life been able to play two against three correctly. My teacher admits he can't count it either; he wants me to play it as he does — by ear."

This confession came, not from a child, but from a teacher of long standing, with years of experience. She seemed to have no idea of rules governing rhythms of two against three, or, in fact, of rules of any kind, any kind of rhythm.

"You surprise me when you say your professor cannot count this himself nor show you how to do it."

"Oh, well," she answered, "he's all right, and such a fine player!"

I gave her a little diagram, using the common multiple of two and three — six. If we count six to each triplet, the notes fall on one — three — five; while the twos are played on one and four. In a moment she saw the scheme, and the problem which had been a life-long puzzle to her, was solved.

"I am so thankful to know how to do this," she said. "I have been told any number of stories about the composers and their music; I have been taught the poetical side, but not the practical side. In short, I have been taught music but not musicianship. Is there any book I can get that will teach me rhythm and how to count?"

I advised her to count aloud when she practiced, to procure a metronome and learn how to use it. Also to study carefully Mr. A. K. Virgil's work on Foundational Training, using a metronome for all rhythmical exercises.

CHAPTER V

TOUCH AND TONE

GETTING RESULTS WITH TONE

A BUSINESS man writes:

" I am puzzled to account for the kind of tone that different players obtain from the piano. In my business I meet a lot of piano players, of all kinds, some of them very good, others the reverse. They will play on the very same piano; some will produce a rich, mellow quality of tone, others a thin, hard tone. In fact each player seems to have a different touch and tone, while the same instrument will not sound twice alike. It's not always the highest class player who will draw out the best tone, either. Quite an ordinary chap — maybe a child — may bring out a quality that those higher up seem to lack. I wish you could enlighten me."

The reason these various persons make the piano sound so differently is because they touch it quite differently, that is their arms, wrists and fingers are in different condition. A good piano is very responsive and obeys whatever the hand or the thought wills. The player with stiff arms, unyielding wrists and iron fingers will only draw cold, hard tones. He pounds,

125

punches or hits the keys and they give back the same vicious quality. Another with relaxed arms, pliable wrists, fingers that are vitally alive to what they are doing, will bring out a beautiful, rich, mellow quality of tone. Such a player can make the piano whisper, thunder or sing with true sympathetic touch. No matter how loudly he plays, the tone is never harsh, but deep and full. For the piano is a very human affair after all, and gives back, with interest, whatever you put into it.

Now what is this secret? If every player could discover it, would you not think each one would want to secure it for himself? In one word, it is the management of the arm. As the violinist considers the bow arm gives him his power of expression and nuance, so it is with the pianist. It is his arm that controls the quality of tone. The arm is the reservoir of power. The more power needed, the more he throws on the arm weight; the less power needed, the more the weight is held up and suspended. But always there is some relaxed weight used, enough to color the quality of tone.

I have a young pupil of musical instincts, though really not gifted. Yet she has grasped the principle of arm weight, so that her tone is at all times of mellow, sympathetic quality. In this respect, it surpasses that of other students, who may practice five times more daily, and are far in advance of her in musicianship.

Whoever will acquire a beautiful singing qual-

ity of tone at the piano, should look to the arm
and note its condition and movement. If it is
held stiffly at the side, not free and relaxed, there
is the answer as to why the tone is not rich and
full. Liberate the arm and watch the tone improve.

TONE PRODUCTION ON THE PIANO

" Pianists think little or nothing about tone
and tone production on the piano," said a prominent vocalist to me the other day. " The tones
of the piano are already fixed — made for them;
they think if they hit the right ones, when playing, it is all they have to do. With the singer
the case is entirely different. She is obliged to
make the tone — it is a part of herself; the ap-
paratus used to make it is hidden, it cannot be
seen; therefore she has got to *think* tone before
it can be produced. Thought is absolutely necessary to the singer when making tones, whereas
any one can hit keys on the piano and make
sounds."

Every teacher of the piano will feel this criticism is just. The very ease with which keys are
depressed blinds the student to the necessity for
careful study into the manner of tone production.
How many students really listen to the sounds
they are making? They look out for wrong
notes, but that is about as far as thought goes.
As for testing the *quality* of the tones in the
melody they are playing, of following the melodic
line with the right kind of shading, of finishing

the phrase tastefully and not with a *sforzando,* students prove to us daily, by the way they play, that they seldom give these things a thought. As for having a mental concept of the tone quality of the phrase or melody clearly defined in mind before the fingers come in contact with the keys, such a thought is incomprehensible to the average pupil.

This can be explained in two ways: First, because they cannot read the page of music, as the singer can, and gain the least idea of " how it sounds," and, second, they have never made a study of tone production at the instrument.

Surely piano instruction needs a reform in this direction. It is a good thing to impress upon pupils to listen to their own playing; but this, of itself, does not go far enough — is not sufficient. *What must they listen for?*

Let us see. First single tones, each to be studied for its own quality of beauty. Next, pairs of tones, the first heavier, the second lighter, representing the perfect phrase. Trills all varieties of tone color. Octaves and chords are to be treated in the same way, for evenness, solidity and variety. Teach your pupils not only to *listen,* but *what to listen for.*

WHAT IS THE MATTER WITH YOUR TOUCH?

I am continually having pupils come to me "passionately fond of music," as they say, and may have had lessons for any number of years. But can they play? Can they speak with their

fingers? Alas, their touch is so weak and ineffective that it can be said they make no effect
at all.

What is wrong with the touch? Various
things. Here is a *dead* touch, with no vitality
or brightness in it. What is the trouble with
it? *The player holds his fingers on, or close to
the keys;* there is no finger action, no development of knuckle joints; result — everything
sounds dull and monotonous,— on a dead level.

What is the remedy? Principles of Condition and Movement must be studied at once.
Touch must be made vital and alive through
distinct and exact finger movements. The
player must go back to first principles and correct this fault.

Other players have the opposite fault; they
play with a sharp, hard tone. Indeed the tone
is so strident it almost gives physical pain to
listen to it. What is the trouble here and how
shall it be corrected? Stiff wrists, contracted
arms and general tense conditions are to blame.
The remedy is to loosen up arms and wrists and
to acquire relaxed arm weight on the key. Cultivate a *live* touch if you would play effectively
and make your playing vital.

THE FASHION OF IT

Years ago it was the fashion to play the piano
with a light, superficial touch, using the fingers
principally, some hand action at the wrist, but
with arms and elbows remaining quiet, almost

stationary at the sides of the body. This manner of playing had a long vogue; even now in many small towns and cities there are people who teach and play in this stiff, constrained, cold manner.

Those who are wide awake, who keep up with the times, have learned to use their wings — otherwise arms. They have learned freedom of movement, learned to make the whole body supple, to use relaxed weight of arm, to play with power and depth of tone, in place of the meaningless tinkling of other days.

We must cultivate expressive touch on the piano. Teachers are beginning to realize this more and more. Yet every teacher will testify to the difficulty of getting pupils to play with sufficient decision of touch, necessary power and meaning. Said one teacher, whose home is in a small southern city:

"We don't seem to play the piano where I come from as you do here in the North; we seem to lack the decision, the vigor of touch you deem so necessary."

"But the great pianists play in your town or vicinity; in listening to them you learn what power, expressive touch and tonal variety may accomplish." She did not seem convinced, however, that a good deal more effort was necessary.

Let me repeat — it is no longer the fashion to play the piano in a weak, ineffective, sentimental manner. The "old order" has departed, "giving place to the new." We now look for round, full‘ tone, clear distinct touch, plenty of light and shade, power and effect. The whole body becomes pliant — through the new order of study, and all necessary muscles are brought into use. Piano playing has a far deeper meaning than it used to have. It is a vital means of self expression; as such it requires vigor and decision of touch and tone, in order to voice the emotional intensity contained in the music, and in ourselves. For we are learning to make piano music *speak*, therefore we must possess an expressive touch.

"PLAYING WITH STYLE"

Do you not find that students often come to their lessons with the notes of their pieces correctly learned, it may be, but rendering them in such a wooden, constrained, cramped fashion that the utterance — as music — is well-nigh unintelligible? Just as though a student of French should recite a page of Racine, pronounce all the words, but with no idea of their meaning. Although the words are spoken their meaning is hidden, buried in the letter — for the spirit is lacking. Not only is there no meaning in the playing of such students, but there is no balance of parts, no symmetry, architecture nor atmosphere. The piece reminds one of a pile of blocks, thrown together with little idea of form or design. And yet the player may have in his repertoire quite a list of pieces, all probably in about the same condition, which he has even memorized. He assures you he is eager to play well and "with style."

Style in piano playing, I take it, means the giving to each composition the required touch, tone, tempo, dynamics and expression which will best express its meaning and content.

How shall we enable the student to understand these things?

It is probable the sort of a pupil referred to has played fast, with little attention to detail. He must now learn to play slowly, pick the composition apart, analyze its keys, cadences, structure and so on. Then the parts are reunited and viewed as a whole. The rhythm must also be correct, for nothing distorts the piece so much as faulty time and rhythm. Finally search for the high lights of the picture and bring these forward, subduing the less important parts.

In a case like the above, it is better to give some simple music, even though the student feels himself equal to cope with difficult pieces. He may indeed be able to play a complex arrangement of notes, but the ability to set forth the inner meaning contained in those notes lags behind.

Among short pieces suitable for such cases, may be mentioned Chopin's Preludes Nos. 7, 10 and 20. Grieg's Papillons is another piece from which to learn a fine and delicate style. This last is often more or less ruined by heavy, ruthless hands.

A few numbers played interestingly, with a

just conception of the appropriate style required for each, is far better than running through a quantity of difficult music, with little idea of its meaning, and less ability to render that meaning expressively.

On the subject of playing with style, a young teacher writes:

"I have great trouble to get my children to play with any style. Most of my pupils are juniors from six to fourteen. But I feel they should learn to put some style into their work. How shall I go about this?"

One cannot advise children to play with style, and let it go at that. How shall young children even have an idea what the word means? The teacher must herself have a pretty clear notion of the meaning of the term; at least she must know some of the attributes of style. Have you a clear concept of the word and its elements? Have you thought out whether it can be dissected and analyzed,— what may be the component parts of that elusive word — style?

Let us see. First of all there must be command of the fundamental forms of touch, legato, staccato, non-legato and portamento. How can any degree of style be acquired if this understanding and command are lacking? Second; Accent plays a large part in the acquisition of an interesting style. Accent gives point and emphasis to everything you play. An orator would be too monotonous to endure, if he had no command of emphasis, and it is the same when we speak with our fingers. And we must continually realize we *can* speak intelligently with our fingers, and say something worth while.

Third, light and shade enter largely into forming one's style of playing. Crescendo and diminuendo — loud and soft, with every conceivable tint between, should be within the player's grasp. The aim should be to make the extremes of loud and soft as wide apart as possible, so that we shall obtain many more shades on the tonal palette.

Then what of the pedals, the very soul of the piano? Your larger children will learn something of their use.

Before one can hope to acquire style in piano playing, one must have some such preparation as is indicated above. Only the principal points are mentioned, but they will doubtless give the player and teacher hints to work upon. It is urged that the ambitious teacher cultivate those qualities of touch, tone and technic in pupils, which belong to the foundation upon which a musical and expressive style is built.

CULTIVATING TOUCH

A teacher writes:

" I have as pupil, a young lady of twenty-five, who recently came to me. She seems to have no idea of touch. How shall I make this subject plain to her? She has stiff knuckles."

You would not attempt to use a machine that creaked in the joints and hinges, and would not *run,* without first oiling and putting it in order. Your pupil's hands are like a rusty, unused machine; they need to be exercised and limbered up. Give her various table exercises, studies in finger action and arm dropping. Principles of touch can be learned at the table, then applied to passage work, études and pieces. Two of the leading touches — legato and staccato — should first be analyzed, thoroughly understood, then worked out in technical form, scales and short pieces. The Brooklet, by Heller, is a good example of legato touch, while the short Tarantelle of Mendelssohn, Number 45 of Songs without Words, will give staccato effects.

TONAL PERSPECTIVE IN PIANO PLAYING

A great orchestral leader spoke to the writer recently of the concept of tonal perspective which the performer of a musical composition must have in order to present the work in correct proportion.

"It is like looking at a picture," he said; "you see the various objects represented, some are in the foreground and catch the eye first; others are in middle distance, not perceived so readily, while others again are set far back in the distance and are quite misty and shadowy. It would be quite unnatural if the far away distance were painted very distinctly and the foreground shadowy. Objects must be set in correct relation to each other, or the whole effect is destroyed."

An illustration of perfect perspective may be drawn from the performance of that super pianist, Josef Hofmann. To-day he played a marvelous recital, in which every variety of expression, every shade of tonal coloring were present; through these means the perspective was perfect. The second illustration is taken from the playing of a local pianist, who played in public recently. The tone was of one monotonous color and loudness, with scarcely any light and shade. Naturally, clearness and accent were also lacking. Yet the friendly audience applauded the efforts of this ill equipped player.

This is the trouble with much of the piano playing heard from students; it has no perspective. Important objects in the musical picture are topsy turvy, all out of shape and proportion. Prominent themes are not brought out, while parts that should be subdued and kept in the background, are too pronounced. So you see the pianist needs to have some idea of architecture in order to arrange the musical structure according to just proportion. He should at every opportunity study good drawing and painting, that he may grow in comprehension of perspective and color.

To acquire the ability to bring out one voice and subdue others, no one thing will do more for the student than the study of Bach. This study can be begun very early, with the First Lessons in Bach, by Walter Carroll, or Mac-Dowell. Then come the charming Bach Dances,

selected from various Suites and Partitas.
Along with this goes the study of lyric music.
There is a storehouse to be found in Mendelssohn's Songs without Words. A few of these,
carefully analyzed, absorbed and memorized, will
do much toward cultivating the feeling for tonal
perspective in piano playing.

PRINCIPLES APPLIED

"I have had an endless amount of technical
work shown me by various teachers," said a
bright woman, who has a large class of pupils
during the season, but during vacation was ea-
gerly seeking light on the principles of piano
playing and teaching. These clever technics
are like so many unattached devices which it
is pleasant to know about, but which one cannot very well use, that is, if the principles underlying them are not perfectly clear. An artist-
teacher may play a piece for you, telling you of
the particular effects he makes here and there,
but, alas, does not tell you the one important
thing you want to know, namely, just how to
make that effect. You look over the various
devices you have been shown from time to time,
wondering if any of them will do. What are
they good for, these interesting technical stunts,
which you have gained from high-priced
teachers? Are they merely "pictures to hang
on memory's walls," or are they of practical
value? You would exchange them all for a few
vital principles, and the knowledge which would

help you apply those principles to touch and tone, and to the pieces you are studying. If it is a good working idea, built on common sense, and practical, you can use it; if you do not, or cannot apply it, there is not much value for you in it.

Suppose you have heard a great deal about relaxed arm weight, exact finger action, flexible wrists, the various touches for legato, staccato, marcato and the like. Suppose, further, that you can even do technical exercises illustrating these principles; but if you do not apply this knowledge to pieces of what real use is it? It will not make your pieces more effective, if you do not use it. You may think this a strange statement, but I have seen it verified over and over again. You can, perhaps, play chord forms with quite good touches; shall you throw to the winds this ability when you attempt pieces? You learned the technical form in order to make the piece effective. But you must *apply* the principle. This requires clear thinking; but clear thinking is required to get anywhere with anything. My advice to all who aspire to become good players and teachers is: Seek out the teacher who can put before you the principles which underlie effective touch and tone in artistic piano playing; who can also give you the right ideas about applying them. Then use your mind and *get there!*

SPEAK WITH CONVICTION

"Be sure you're right; then go ahead," is a good maxim to follow. The teacher of piano, to be successful, must thoroughly know what he is trying to teach. He should not only believe in it but absolutely know it is the right way to study. If he not only believes it but knows it, he will make others believe and know it; he will speak with conviction.

It is easy to speak with conviction, if you are sure you are right. It is well, at the season's start, to examine your methods of teaching and study, and see if they are in working order, up-to-date, progressive and thorough. If they are and you are sure of yourself and what you are able to teach, you can speak with authority and your assurance will carry conviction to the mind of the pupil. The pupil will have confidence in what you advise her to do. If she has been badly taught and you can convince her she ought to do certain kinds of technical work to correct her faults, she will listen and obey. Remember she has to take you on trust. You must be so fired by the truth of what you preach and so certain of its effect, that your words carry the necessary conviction. Then *know* what you are talking about, and you will surely speak with authority!

CHAPTER VI

ON MEMORIZING

LEARNING BY HEART

"I AM a young girl just starting out to teach; I want to ask many questions but will content myself with these for the present. What kind of pieces shall I give a beginner? Should they be learned by heart? How shall I teach memorizing?"

There are many pretty and interesting pieces, suitable for the first year. Thomé has several "Melodies"; there is the Album for the Young, Schumann; Theme and Variations, Mozart; little pieces by Grieg, Rheinhold, Lange, Mrs. Adams, Florence Barbour and many others. Use good music; even though simple it should be interesting and express some thought. Do not give too difficult pieces, a common fault. See that there is nothing in the piece you are giving that has not been prepared for in the technical exercises.

I teach memorizing from the first lesson. To learn by heart is the most thorough and practical kind of learning, for then only do you *know* what you are studying. Teach your young pupils to memorize their earliest technical exercises. They are to recite the notes and fingering of each hand alone. When these are perfectly understood and can be correctly played each hand alone, they are taken together. If it be a small melodic figure, repeated over and over, up and down the piano, the plan of it is probably simple enough. The notes and fingering of first figure are recited, the rest is only repetition. Treat the little étude and piece in the same way. Notice how many measures are alike in the piece, and how many are varied: how many measures are formed from the common chords of the scale. Help your pupils to analyze their pieces and see that they understand the triads of each scale. This is done through a systematic recitation of these triads. With étude or piece, it is one measure at a time, one hand at a time. Recite, Learn, Think, Play, Listen!

HOW DO YOU MEMORIZE YOUR PROGRAM?

A pianist writes:

"I am having trouble in committing my program. I try to gain a mental concept of the portion to be memorized before playing it, and the result seems good for the time being, but it is not permanent. Of course I realize years are necessary to acquire a repertoire, and I believe I have the patience, if I know how to work."

Two thoughts occur to me as I read your letter. How, or by what method do you learn by heart; the necessity of repetition.

1. How is your memorizing done? You say

you try to "gain a mental concept of the portion to be memorized before playing it." Do you learn each hand separately and then put them together? Do you analyze the portion under consideration for keys, chord progressions and construction; do you know them so well you can recite the notes of each? The whole thing in a nutshell is simple enough: either you know the piece or you do not; either you know each note, each mosaic or you do not.

About the most thorough way to learn the notes, is to memorize them away from the piano. Then you are shut up to a mental concept, and are not distracted by the sound of keys or outward movements. These also have to be learned, but the process of learning notes is a thing apart; it must always be done first if you are trying to commit the piece to memory.

Repetition. Do not think, because you have once learned the piece so that you can go through it respectably, that it will stay put forever. One must always keep his repertoire in repair. Read "Piano Mastery," and see what many artists have to say on this point. Some pianists believe in going over their repertoire once a week, to see that everything is all right. This does not mean merely *playing* the pieces, but rather going over them carefully and slowly, with the printed page before you. You need to refresh your memory as to how those notes look on the printed page, what the signs of expression and dynamics are and so on. Every artist does this constantly, especially before a recital. I remember seeing a well known pianist studying the pages of his concerto, before he stepped upon the platform to play with orchestra. Calling upon Mme. Teresa Carreno, on one occasion, all the music for her recital the following day was piled on the piano, although she had but just arrived in town. She traveled with those pieces — never went anywhere without them.

Therefore do not be discouraged because your pieces will not always stick in memory. Find out the weak spots in each piece, and make them good. Note, in each repetition, what was faulty, unclear, inartistic, and make a special study of that place.

" My pieces are all scarred over with accident blots," lamented an ambitious player, who sometimes got into trouble when playing for others, through nervousness.

" Say rather, your pieces are dotted over with victories," was the answer. If we will but look at the matter in this light, it is more than likely we shall score a victory of some kind every time.

SHALL YOUNG PUPILS MEMORIZE?

A young teacher asks whether very young pupils should be taught to memorize and whether they should be assisted in doing so.

I certainly believe young pupils should be taught to learn by heart. Why should they not begin from the very start the training for this very important branch of musical equipment?

It is not difficult to encourage, from the very first lesson, such concentration that they begin to commit the first simple table exercises shown them. Expect them to learn these forms, require them to do so. By requiring this you are laying the foundation for the future memorizing of a Beethoven Sonata or a Chopin Nocturne. Certainly help them with the first piece, as you have helped them from the very start; show them how the piece is put together, how to find its sections and how to learn each part. Train your pupils to thoughtful habits of attention and memory, and expect them to keep right on.

CHAPTER VII

FOR PIANO STUDENTS

WHY DO YOU STUDY MUSIC?

THIS question is sometimes put to the new student. The answers are apt to be various. One says: "I take lessons because I want to play the latest dance music." Another says: "I want to know how to play well, for when I am invited anywhere one feels awkward if one knows nothing of piano music." Yet another wishes to learn the piano to please Father and Mother, in the home circle. Then there are many who study with the object of becoming teachers. There are others, alas! who merely drift along, with no object before them.

I would like to say to each one who takes up piano study: Have an object in that study. Do nothing aimlessly. If you are learning for your own pleasure, use it as a means of self-improvement; for music is the most inspiring branch of study you can undertake. If you only wish to play the latest dances, you need well-developed fingers and a reliable sense of rhythm, also ability to read at sight. If you wish to please your friends when you are invited out, you must cultivate your technic, acquire a musical, expressive touch and a knowledge of salon composition. If your aim is to cheer and elevate the home circle, no effort is too great for such a labor of love. In any case music must be well played or it will give no pleasure; if it is not, your object will be defeated. And lastly, if you expect to teach, you are compelled to learn everything, from the foundation up, very thoroughly, in order to be able to direct others, and to become a teacher worthy the name. You cannot point the way to others unless you know it yourself.

So there is no getting away from the obligation to learn whatever you attempt in music with whole-hearted enthusiasm. And above all, have a high aim in whatever you undertake.

THAT UNKNOWN THUMB JOINT

I recently questioned a large class of advanced students of piano upon the first principles of piano playing. Among the questions I put was one so simple I almost hesitated to ask it.

"How many joints have the fingers?" They all knew that, and answered, three.

"Very good," I said; "and the thumb — how many joints has the thumb?"

They were not at all ready with this answer. Some thought the thumb had two joints, while others decided in favor of one!

This result did not surpirse me. In all my career as teacher of piano, I can count on the fingers of one hand the students who have come to me prepared to answer this question correctly. It matters not how many years pupils have studied, or with what great personalities, they still seem to be in utter ignorance of the fact that the thumb has *three* joints, just as the other fingers have. This very ignorance proves they seldom *think,* seldom consider the machine which they possess, in order to learn what can be done with it, or what can be made out of it. The knowledge that there is a knuckle joint at the base of the thumb at once changes the manner of using that member, and liberates its movement. With the thumb free and independent, we possess, as it were, another finger. I wish it were possible to awaken every student, who is trying to learn the piano, to the importance of knowing the fundamentals, and how to use the hand in playing. Among the " first things " to be learned, is the truth about the acting joint of the fingers, that is — where they move from.

Let us realize we have five fingers on each hand and train them according to correct principles. Let us give extra attention to the thumb, whose knuckle joint has been so long neglected and ignored. Let us cultivate this joint and free the thumb from its long captivity.

WHAT THE PUPIL SHOULD DO FOR HIMSELF

Every teacher knows how much of the lesson time must often be spent in correcting errors that should never be made, or should be eliminated by the pupil at home. Wrong notes, faulty

rhythm or incorrect fingering should never be
brought to the teacher, for these are things the
pupil himself can prevent. Why should he pay
a teacher to do the work for him? It is unfair
to both. On the pupil's part, it proves inatten-
tion and carelessness — a lack of concentration
during practice.

If you are studying music, the best way to help
yourself and please your teacher is to bring the
material given you as well prepared as your present knowledge permits; at least you can bring
it free from wrong notes, wrong fingering and
wrong time. In other words you must play correct notes in perfect time, and with correct fingering. Your teacher can then give his undi-
vided attention to interpretation and effect.
You will thus gain the whole benefit of his wide
experience and knowledge.

"LEND ME YOUR EARS"

"Lend me your ears!" was the appeal of Bru-
tus with which he opened his oration over the
body of his friend Julius Cæsar.

Every time the student presents himself for
a lesson, he silently and all unconsciously repre-
sents the same thought — lend me your ears.
He has come to have the use of his teacher's
ears for the prescribed hour. The teacher lends
his ears, together with all his knowledge and
experience, to correct the faults of the pupil and
give him all possible aid and advice.

When you come to your teacher — perhaps at

the end of the day — you may not consider how severe a whole day of " ear-lending " may have been. For all those hours the instructor has been on the alert, listening for various shades of tone quality, for wrong notes, faulty phrasing, incorrect fingering, ineffective and unmusical performance. He must listen every moment with entire concentration. He must get the perspective and see the complete picture. Only understanding and experience enable the teacher to so listen and to criticize with judgment.

There is the other side. The student must learn to cultivate his own ears, so that he shall be able to criticize himself. The teacher shows him how, then bids him go and put the knowledge gained into practice during the week. Thus to cultivate our sense of hearing up to the finest point is about the most important thing we can do in our music study.

CURE FOR THE STOPPING HABIT

The unfortunate habit of interrupting the continued flow of the piece by stopping short in various places in it, is more prevalent than one would think. It assails all kinds of players, from beginners to those far advanced, and is a serious drawback to any sort of artistic performance.

The causes behind this habit are several. The beginner stumbles through his first piece, making breaks here and there, because he has not been taught to go " straight through " every technical passage or study, from the very first lesson on. As he advances, he learns to analyze his piece and commits it to memory in sections — fragments. It is not strange that he is not always ready to remember which part comes next, hence the tendency to hesitate, and at times, to stop.

There should be a remedy for this state of things — and there is! Slow practice with metronome will be of great benefit. That piece which you hesitate and stumble over, should be taken much more slowly, with metronome, and played straight through. This does not mean that difficult places should not be worked out in detail and repeated many times. It does mean, however, that part of each day's practice should include the " straight through " plan. The same can be applied to the review pieces you are keeping up. If you are unaccustomed to the metronome, this advice may be a little difficult to follow at first. But it must be done if you are ever to master that piece and others like it.

The trouble is, you did not begin the " straight through " plan when you first began to study music. That should have been done at the first lesson. If you had played each exercise from beginning to end without a fault — made a practice of doing so from the start, you would have no troubles of this kind now.

But it is never too late to mend one's ways. Start at once performing your technical stunts without a mistake; treat pieces in the same way. Learn to go straight through — often with metronome; after a little time you will be able to conquer this annoying fault.

SHALL WE HAVE SLOW OR FAST PRACTICE?

Dr. William Mason, one of our famous American teachers, used to say that not one student in twenty knew how to practice, because not one in twenty was willing to practice slowly enough. "I had rather the pupil would bring me one page, thoroughly and carefully learned, than ten pages carelessly and superficially gone over. The trouble with American pupils is they practice too fast and not carefully and correctly." A number of pianists now before the public testify to fondness for slow practice. One said to me yesterday: "I always play very slowly. Even when I know the piece and am reviewing it for concert, I work at it slowly, because otherwise there will be errors and slips. And it must be more than a hundred per cent. sure. There are often disturbances mental and otherwise, going on when one is playing for others or in public, and one cannot afford to be uncertain in the smallest particular."

And yet the student appears to know much more than the masters, because he insists on playing fast; therefore he constantly stumbles and makes mistakes, unless continually held in check by the teacher. Here is where the metronome is an invaluable aid, which no pupil should be without. Slow, careful practice will — or should — insure correctness in three things; notes, time, fingering. If the pupil fails in any one of them at his lesson, the cause is at once found to be — fast practice. Then let us have by all means Slow Practice!

ASKING QUESTIONS

How many students are wide awake enough to ask the teacher questions? You might thus learn much. What is the reason of your silence at the lesson? Are you afraid to betray your ignorance by asking; are you indifferent and don't care about knowing; or do you think your duty done if you go to your lesson and passively wait to be told everything?

You have never thought how it would cheer your teacher if you show enough interest to ask questions. The great teacher, Leschetizky used to say to those stolid ones, " Why don't you talk? How can I tell whether you understand me unless you ask questions? " Remember you can " draw out " your teacher and obtain more light on your work. Don't fear your teacher will not like to be questioned. She will like you a great deal better for the interest you show, for you prove you are thinking. Your teacher does not greatly care for the pupil who has no curiosity about the thing she pretends to study.

If some one should come to you one day with a document, proving you to be the owner of a beautiful estate, which was awaiting your acceptance, you would ply that person with end-less questions as to *what* the place was like, *where* it was and *how* you could get there. For you would not passively accept such an amazing piece of news in silence, showing no interest in it.

You can have a possession all your own in the land of music, if you are anxious enough to learn how to get there.

A LURKING DANGER

Students often make the mistake of trying to imitate the positions and movements at the keyboard of some great artist they may have heard. If the artist holds his hands quite flat at times, with little or no finger movements, the student thinks it will be more artistic and far easier, to play in the same way. So he begins to lay aside all finger action and let his hands and fingers flop about quite carelessly, as he thinks by so doing he may be able to play like the artist.

No doubt the teacher of this student has been at great pains to cultivate finger action, teaching him to arch the hand, curve fingers and play with accurate movements. But the student, thinking he knows better, especially after seeing the artist play with absolute control and no effort, concludes he will not take the trouble to lift his fingers, since the artist's way is much simpler.

What is the result? The student's playing

soon becomes uncertain and smeary, his tone weak and muddy, his playing ineffective. He may get through a modern salon piece, using a good deal of pedal; but he never can play Mozart, or any music of clear-cut form and variety of tonal shading.

A teacher remarked to me lately: "I have a young pupil, a boy, whom I have taught very carefully; he has good finger movements and played with clean clear touch. He was away all summer; when he returned he was almost ruined; my work has now to be done all over again. He met a young fellow during the summer who played brilliantly but very carelessly, with flat fingers and no action at the knuckle joint, to speak of. My boy thought it a good thing to imitate, and this is the result. I only hope I can get him back into right ways again, but it will be hard work."

Students, beware of this lurking danger.

A WORD TO THE BOYS

A young man connected with the business of music, in a capacity where a good working knowledge of music is not only an advantage but an essential, recently remarked:

"If I had my boyhood to live over again, I would study music thoroughly. To my shame I have to confess that I had my chance and did not improve it. My good parents gave me the opportunity of piano lessons, but I didn't appreciate them. How I used to hate that practice hour! I used to turn the hands of the clock ahead, to shorten it. I never realized it was the most foolish thing I could do. I never imagined the time would come when I would bitterly regret such laziness and deceit. At the present moment, I would give almost anything I possess to have the knowledge I might have gained in those early years. I feel like exhorting every boy I meet not to make the mistake I made then."

That boy is very short-sighted who will neglect the valuable and ennobling study of music, when the chance is given him to pursue it. Like the speaker above quoted, the opportunity may come to him in a few years, to make use of his musical knowledge in ways he never, as a boy, could foresee. His business may become fifty per cent. more valuable and lucrative through an understanding of music. And even if he have no need to use it commercially, he may have daily use for it from a higher standpoint. Both as boy and man, music will help mold, soften, refine and spiritualize his character.

The American boy, up to now, seems to have had the idiotic idea that the study of music will make him effeminate. This belief may be a relic of days gone by, when uninstructed teachers used to give their pupils foolish, silly music. In these days, when teachers and people generally are becoming more enlightened, when the best music can be had in cheap editions, there is no reason for playing trash.

The study of good music will form the boy's

character, and render him open to the finer and higher issues of life and manhood.

HOW MUCH PRACTICE?

A school girl laments the fact she has so little time for practice, since there are so many lessons on other subjects to be learned outside of school hours. Many other girls, she says, have the same difficulty, and asks what they shall do.

One should practice at least one hour a day, in order to make even a little progress. Though you may consider your day well filled, there may be several half hours unaccounted for, or that may be secured with care and forethought. One will be yours by rising an hour earlier in the morning. Time may also be gained on the way to and from school, which may be used in thinking out the piece you are trying to memorize. Real practice does not consist in sitting before the keyboard a certain length of time each day, but of mental effort and concentration. The mind must work more than the fingers; it can work no matter where the body happens to be. Never forget that. An illustration of what can be done in music, even though one is in school, is drawn from a pupil of mine who attended school, did some housework, yet found time to devote three hours daily to piano practice. Truly where there's a will there's a way, when the student is talented, ambitious, ready to work and eager for success.

PLAYING FOR OTHERS

A student writes:

" I want your advice on a matter which has always troubled me. I am able to memorize and play pretty well when alone, but when playing for others I lose self-control and often play miserably. Do you think this fault is curable? It is mighty discouraging, I assure you, when one feels one really *can* do things. I shall be happy to know of a remedy."

There should be a remedy for this disastrous condition, and in your case I am sure there is! But it comes from hard work — with yourself. You evidently see the trouble is a mental one, for it is only " when playing for others " that you fail. The trouble is lack of concentration and self-control. The remedy is the acquisition of these qualities. When Josef Hofmann or Jascha Heifetz — to name two of the greatest artists of the present day — come before an audience, they are absolutely self-contained and absorbed in what they are doing. The piece they are playing is the most vital and absorbing thing in the world to them; the present moment the most serious and momentous of the whole day. If you would be always at your best, consider your work at all times with the utmost seriousness, and for the time being, the performance of it the one thing in the world of importance. You must keep your thought on what you are doing, or you can never do it

worthily. Fear of failure must never come in
to disturb you; this fear paralyzes clear thinking.

Now this concentration I speak of cannot be
gained over night. But it can be begun to-day;
it must be a daily growth. The main thing is
to go through exercise or piece without a mistake. Begin to cultivate this habit to-day.

Another difficulty is that you do not know
the piece thoroughly enough to provide, at every
point, for mishaps. Everything must be analyzed and every detail committed to memory.
There are many ways to do this; each player
will find the one best suited to his needs.

The school in which you acquire concentration
soonest, is in playing for others. Play for some
one every day. Play for your pupils, if you are
teaching, for friends, for every one possible.
The " man in the street " is best, for if you can
make him listen with interest, you can doubtless
please any one.

Finally, keep eternally at it. It is worth
working for, this poise and self-control. If you
keep at it and never yield to discouragement,
you will surely win.

BE READY

We admire the man, or woman either, who is
always ready to act, to speak; who is prepared
for any emergency, who is never taken unawares.
We also admire the young music student who
can always play something at the piano if asked

to do so. This ought to be possible after one year's study. By this time principles of technic have been acquired and several pieces have been studied. Every ambitious pupil is anxious to take as many pieces as the teacher will permit. These, of course, have to be thoroughly learned and committed to memory. Perhaps the student may not care to retain all his earliest pieces, but he will probably have five to show for his year's study. The next season he will learn about ten. If half a dozen of these are kept in review, he will always have something at his finger tips to play, when asked; he will always be ready. Young students of the piano owe it to their parents and teachers to keep a few well liked pieces in readiness to be produced when called upon. Never let your practice fall behind; keep it up for a hundred reasons.

WHAT CONSTITUTES AN ARTIST?

Two ambitious students of our instrument have written, asking this question. We will answer them together.

The first says: "I have studied the piano for a number of years, and am told I have some talent. I am anxious to become an artist. How much time will it take each day, and for how many years?"

The other day a young pianist came to my studio to play for me. She expects to make her debut in six months, and is at work on her program. She practices five hours a day, and had done so daily for the past four years. Three hours daily are given to technic. This includes one hour of scales and arpeggios. Another hour is given to technical forms, a third to Bach or a Chopin étude. This leaves but two hours for repertoire, but evidently this young player deems it of prime importance to practice technic. Her playing was smooth and fluent. The secret of her study, her command of the keyboard, was, she assured me, slow practice. She took every-thing slowly; occasionally, of course, up to tempo.

I have used this little incident to answer the first girl's inquiry as to time and kind of prac-tice. No one can tell you whether you can or cannot become an artist. If I could see and hear you play, I might then be able to determine whether you have the "stuff in you" and are on the right road. Everything enters into the making of an artist. Practice your five hours — under the guidance of a good master. Take daily exercise, read good books on music and other arts; read poetry, hear music, see pictures; live a life that is alive to the best. Do this for three years, then judge of the result.

The second query is more from the standpoint of music appreciation perhaps, than actual per-formance. The writer says:

"In this small town where I live, there is little music, except what we make ourselves. I have never heard a great pianist, an artist like Josef Hofmann, for instance. I would not know what to listen for. Your reply will help several of us."

A great artist's playing is difficult to describe since the complete impression is so complex. He must have a beautiful tone, capable of every shade of color and tone quality, from very loud to very soft; a consummate technic of hand and foot, and above all the power to project the intellectual and emotional content of the music across to the listener.

While listening to the Polish pianist, Josef Hofmann, recently, the following points were noted: 1. Variety of tone; 2. Perfect Rhythm; 3. Simplicity of Style; 4. Buoyancy of Tone Quality; 5. Skill in Building up Emotional Climaxes; 6. Working up Crescendos in Tone; 7. Perfect Balance and Perspective; 8. Mastery of Pedaling.

The only way to listen to great pianists, when deprived of hearing them in concert, is through records of the Duo Art, Ampico or other reproducing instruments. Procure good records and profit by, as well as enjoy their study.

AN INTERESTING LETTER

Here is a letter from a girl who *thinks*, who is serious about her music study. She lives in a little Wisconsin town, which can boast few musical advantages; but she is making the most of those within reach. Her words should inspire any girl or boy to study earnestly and

make something of their music that will be worth
while.   I will quote the letter in full.

"I am a girl of sixteen, a junior in the High
School.   I have always loved music and hope
to make a business of it one day.   I am the only
musical one in our family of eight.   I have
taken three years on the piano, six months on
the violin, and three months singing.   The piano
interests me most of all.   This year I could not
take lessons, as my people could not afford it.
Here are the names of some of my latest pieces:
Beethoven, Sonata, Op. 13; Mozart, Fantaisie
and   Sonata;   Schubert,   Impromptu;   Grieg,
Spring Song; Chopin, Fifteen Valses; Mason,
Technics and Kohler's Daily Repetitions.   My
intention is to work my way through some musical institution when I finish High School.

"Will you kindly answer the following questions?

"1. Do you think I can make a success of
music, the way conditions are?   2. How much
time should I devote each day to music?   3.
Would you have one rest day every week?   4.
How many hours would you devote to technic?
5. What kind of pieces would you choose to
memorize first?   6. What are some good piano
pieces for daily practice?   7. Would you allow
the playing of popular pieces?   8. What time of
day is best for practice?   9. What would be the
first steps in beginning to practice a classical
piece?   10. What is the correct method of memo-

rizing? 11. At what age should one begin to study music? 12. Would you state the limit of daily practice? 13. Is dance music harmful to play? 14. What is the best way to practice exercises?

" I have taken the *Musical Observer* for over a year, and really must say it contains the most interesting material I have ever read. The money I paid for it I earned by playing at a few dances. As soon as I am able, I shall take it again.

" Yours very truly,

" JUANITA D."

Bravo, Juanita! I am sure you will succeed in music, no matter what the conditions are. I am greatly interested in your letter. The questions you ask show that you are wide awake, and are trying to look at the matter from all sides. I will answer them as briefly and directly as possible. You have my answer to the first, which is unhesitatingly, yes! 2. Give whatever time you are able to music study. If you practice three hours daily you will do well, as you have your school lessons to prepare. But remember that sitting at the piano several hours every day is not all of it; you can do much *thinking* away from the instrument. 3. If music is a joy to you, then its study cannot be wearisome; therefore you personally may not need a " rest-day." Those about you may wish you to take a little respite occasionally, and you will know when to gratify their wishes, within reason. 4. Devote to technic about a quarter or a third of your practice time. 5. Always memorize good music. Let it be so good that it will *wear,* so that you will not easily tire of it. 6. As to pieces for daily practice, it is a good plan to select one piece for each technical point; that is to say, for octaves, scales, chords and trills. The Spinning Song, No. 34 of the Songs without Words, by Mendelssohn, is an excellent number to keep in the daily schedule. 7. As to popular pieces, by all means play them if good of their kind. One acquires both grace and rhythmic swing, if one can toss off popular music with effect. But one needs a good technic to make it at all interesting, even to the unmusical listener. 8. Theoretically, in the morning; practically at any hour of the day. 9. Analyze a difficult classical piece, or any piece worth study, for key, meter, themes, melody, accompaniment, principal and secondary parts, and so on. 10. Memorize your piece phrase by phrase, each hand alone first, then together. 11. You ask at what age to begin to study music. The earlier the better; say at five years. There are, however, many things a child can learn about tones and sounds, about using his fingers and so on, before actual piano lessons are attempted. It is the failure to begin at this end and prepare the mind of the little pupil for what is coming that renders the beginning so chaotic in many cases. 12. Four hours of daily practice should be sufficient. 13. Dance music is not harmful to play; it is often entertaining and inspiring. 14. Do some work in chords, scales, trills and octaves every day; also practice Bach regularly. If you have not begun the Two Part Inventions, you can take up those. Finally, I am perfectly sure, if you are industrious the way will open before you, and you will succeed.

HANDS ABOVE THE KEYBOARD

We often hear about the bashful youth who does not know what to do with his hands. One is reminded of him when dealing with the average music student. He also does not know what should become of his hands when his fingers are not occupied with the keys. Many pupils seem to have the idea that when the hand is not employed it can rest in the lap. On the contrary, when the hand is not needed, it should be poised above the keyboard, ready to fall — prepared for what is coming. Just as the pupil is taught to hold unemployed fingers up, so that when they are needed, simply a down movement is used — not a double motion — so it is with the arm. Instead of leaving the hand in lap until the very instant it is wanted — as is the general custom, thereby scrambling for the key or chord, why not hold hand and arm above the keys, to be in constant readiness? This is what the artist does, in nine times out of ten. Pupils should be taught this point and teachers should insist on its being carried out.

NECESSITY FOR SIGHT READING

Perhaps teachers of the piano do not sufficiently realize the importance to the pupil of training in reading at sight. You may say you have no time for this work in the lessons, that there is so much other material to go over and so on. All this may be quite true; yet with a little planning you can often use ten or fifteen minutes of the hour. Begin this work very early, so the child will constantly add to his sight reading ability and will take pleasure in it.

A lady, quite advanced in piano playing, came to me the past season. During the early lessons I put some unknown music before her, but soon saw she was quite unable to read even a simple piece at sight. "I positively cannot do it," she said. "I have never been able to read at sight, therefore it takes me a very long time to puzzle out my pieces, when I take new ones." I would not give it up. Selecting an easy duet, I insisted on her going through it, counting aloud. She did so. I then prescribed sight reading at home. Each lesson she improved. She found a friend to read with her during the week and is now grateful her attention was turned in this direction. One point must always be insisted on, that the student count aloud when reading at sight. Thus the sense of rhythm is ground into the mentality of the pupil, so to speak, and grows with his musical growth.

FINDING A MELODY

A young girl brought me the A flat major Prelude of Chopin for criticism. She had worked at it for some time by herself, and her playing proved she had not learned how to bring out the melody. This is blended with the accompaniment in most cases, and needs special study in order to make the upper voice sing above the other parts. When the Prelude was played for her she viewed it in an entirely different light. She now heard the melody sing through the whole piece; the accompaniment, supported by the bass, formed the background, instead of mixing with the theme, as she had conceived it.

This matter of finding the melody and bringing it out, is a vital one. It is something which distinguishes the artist from the non-artist. The latter may play the notes correctly, but the artist sets them forth in correct relation to each other; he makes some prominent, others secondary; he knows how to bring out the high lights of the picture, and make it truly a thing of beauty as well as a work of art.

For the study of melody playing, Mendelssohn's Songs without Words offer excellent material. Here we have the three parts into which the structure may be divided, viz.: Melody, bass, accompaniment. Each of these three must find their just balance, their relation to each other and to the whole. The melody, or song, as the principal voice, must rise and fall with the right inflection — just as a singer would deliver it. The deep tones of the bass support it and give rhythmic character, while the accompanying middle part is more subdued, but always provides a tonal background, upon which is woven, like the figures of rich tapestry, the vocal theme or design.

To play lyric music intelligently and effectively, needs discriminating touch; good technic, and an ear capable of distinguishing different qualities of tone. You must find the melody before you can bring it out, or hold it up to others.

Seek for melody in everything you play. You will be rewarded by finding many you would otherwise overlook. Bach will teach you to find these oft-times hidden melodies. His music is made up of interlaced themes; to unravel them is a fascinating study.

MUSIC STUDY FOR THE BUSINESS GIRL

Music study as a means of self-expression, as a refining and elevating force, ought to find a place in the daily life of every business girl and business woman. Music is such a beautiful thing, a jewel to be sought and worn by every one who desires to enjoy high and noble things.

The young woman occupied in an office all day often says: "I love music, but have no time to study." Or she says: "If I only had time to take up music, how happy I should be!"

But you have time to take up music. There is scarcely a girl in an office anywhere who cannot give an hour a day to music study. One hour each day would make three hundred and fifty hours a year; truly a fortune of time. How much you can accomplish in it!

Then why not take piano lessons, if you love music so much? Be sure and go to a good concert whenever you can. An orchestral concert by a fine orchestra is a rich emotional experience. There are various books on the development of music, which the business girl will find enlightening and absorbing. In the large cities are lectures on music and many free musical advantages. In small places there are libraries where you can encourage the managers to supply books on music. If you really love music you can teach yourself something about it. Others have done as much. "Where there's a will there's a way."

CHAPTER VIII

POINTS FOR PARENTS TO THINK OF

HOW PARENTS CAN HELP

THERE are a multitude of ways! If I could only reach the ears of all the mothers of a town, whose children are studying music, how I would like to pour into them suggestions which would open their eyes to the many ways in which they can aid the teacher, who is surely doing her best to interest and advance all the young students under her care.

Home study is a great point. If that is not carefully carried on how can satisfactory progress be made? The mother can see that regular hours are kept and lessons well prepared.

Keeping hands in order and nails trimmed are surely marks of neatness and refinement; the teacher knows how often they are disregarded, by younger pupils especially. She knows how often she is obliged to expostulate against sharp, clanking nails. How can piano keys be properly depressed when fingers are guarded by such appendages? Common sense should govern this point. If the child fails to attend to it the mother must. Per contra, the young woman who cares more for her polished, pointed finger nails than she does for her music, will never learn to play the piano decently, no matter how much money is spent on her musical education. Let parents, and those who are wise enough to use common sense, look after these hindrances to advancement, and there will be fewer failures among the students.

MUSIC IN THE HOME

"If my child does not care enough about music to go and practice of her own accord, I shall never drive her to it. I do not believe in *making* a child practice."

It is usually people of affluence who hold such opinions; their children are accustomed to have most of their wishes gratified. No doubt every teacher of music has heard this remark and has had the same difficulty to contend with.

The conscientious teacher, laboring to do her best to interest the child, finds it a serious problem to answer wisely such a remark, often made before the child herself.

A case of such lack of parental influence and authority came under my notice to-day. The pupil, a quiet little girl of eleven, did not know her lesson when the teacher came; in fact she had done but little practice in two weeks. What was the trouble? When questioned, she affirmed she liked her little Mozart piece and her Duvernoy study; she really liked music, if she could only acquire it without practice. Mother was appealed to, and her answer was in the same strain as the one mentioned above. Was she right?

So far as my experience goes, I answer emphatically, No! Children left to themselves, may not prefer to sit in the house and study, when their playmates are enticing them to come out and play. Shall this childish desire be gratified at the expense of all study and discipline? Shall they go to school with unlearned lessons, simply because they had rather play than study? The wide-awake teacher of piano is striving to teach music along educational lines, as thoroughly as arithmetic and geography are taught in school. What would be thought of the mother who allowed her child to appear in school day after day with lessons unprepared? Would not the child be right later to complain of neglect of authority. "You should have compelled me to study," would be the verdict. The same applies to music. "If I had only been made to practice when I was a small child, how happy I should be now!" is a remark often heard from those who have been thus neglected in early youth.

O mothers and fathers, I beg that this charge may not be laid at your door! Give your children the benefit of musical instruction; encourage them to learn something of this great art. By informing yourself on the subject and by looking after their practice in order that it shall be conscientiously performed, you will be lay-

ing the foundation for much happiness and bless-
ing for your children, for now and always.

LOOKING AHEAD

The child of eight or ten, who begins music
study, has not the faintest idea of what these
lessons may lead to. She has no notion she has
started on a wonderful journey; she cannot guess
the far-reaching effect on her future life and
destiny. But her parents are able to look further ahead. They can even foresee that the
daughter may have a real talent, and may be
called upon to support herself, or to make a
career in music.

With such possibilities ahead, is it not wisdom
to look very carefully after the little student's
work, her practice, her instrument, her teacher?
This is the privilege of the parents, especially
the mother. The idea that any sort of a teacher
will do for a beginner, has long ago — it is
hoped — given place to the right idea, that the
beginner needs the best possible training.

So, if you are looking ahead for good results,
you must start aright. First secure a teacher
who knows how to teach, how to interest the
pupil in the essentials of music study. See that
the instrument is in good order and kept in tune.
Also that the room is light and warm, cheerful
and quiet. Then practice should be a pleasure
instead of the drudgery it often is. Make music
study attractive in every possible way; the re-

ward for your foresight will follow in due course.

A prominent concert pianist said to me the other day:

"Children, especially boys, should be made to practice, if they are allowed to have music lessons. This is the only way — I can speak from experience. I didn't love to practice; in fact, I almost hated it, but I was not allowed to rule. It is sheer nonsense to leave the matter to children, and expect they will go to the piano themselves, without being encouraged or required to do so. Children do not know what they want; they are not capable of judging what is good for them. They must be directed and guided."

A COUPLE OF HINTS TO PARENTS

"I can't practice after lunch because father likes to rest in the room where the piano is," said a bright girl who loves music, but has only a brief time in the day to devote to her music outside of school hours. Another girl said if she could only have the hour from five to six for practice she would be perfectly happy, as that was the hour she could best spare from school studies. But unfortunately, that was just the hour in which the family gathered in the parlor for a chat, so quiet work was impossible.

No doubt, in thousands of homes all over the land, just such conditions exist. While teachers desire to hold the pupil up to earnest effort, insisting that he make the best use of time and opportunity, is it just to expect or require him to do this when so many obstacles are put in his path? Clearly it is not right, it is all wrong.

In the first case we have cited, the father could have rested just as well in another room — there were plenty at his disposal; in the second, the family could have gathered in another part of the house.

"At what tempo do you play this study?" asks the teacher.

" I did not play it with the metronome, for my metronome isn't fixed yet," answered the pupil.

" But you have said the same thing for weeks; last week I wrote a reminder in your record book, so that you would be sure and remember to tell mother."

" Yes, I told her, but she has been too busy to look after it."

No doubt every teacher meets with these experiences. They show the apathy parents often exhibit in attending to the child's musical needs.

If mother's sewing machine is out of order she has it repaired at once. Father sees to it that his tools of whatever nature are in perfect condition. Yet the little music student, struggling with her time-problems, must be left to herself and her needs ignored. Will parents awake to this point?

AN APPEAL

We want men and women all over this great land of ours who will interest themselves in their children's music study. We want mothers who will take the time and the trouble to see how their girls and boys employ their practice hours — mothers who know how practice hours should be spent. We want mothers who realize the value of music as a refining, ennobling, uplifting force for good; mothers who are too well informed to tolerate "rag-time," and too much in earnest to employ fake or charletan teachers. Until we can change the attitude of many 'American parents toward the study of music, we may talk and labor in vain. This is the crying need of this country — parents who know the value of music as a potent factor in education and in character building, who desire its advantages for their children, who are willing to give thought and care to see that the children have competent instruction and are pursuing their studies conscientiously. How many fathers believe their entire obligation consists in meeting the bills when they come due? How many mothers think it necessary to look after the children's practice, or are even capable of doing so? We want parents who will do more than merely pay bills! If we have not this sort in America, the obligation rests with those of us who know better, to help in some way to educate the unfortunate "others," and bring them to some way to educate the unfortunate "others," and bring them to some comprehension of what is lacking and what is needed.

CHAPTER IX

QUESTIONS AND ANSWERS

AGE AND MUSIC STUDY

"I AM eighty-seven years old and became interested in music in the form of song six years ago. I have just bought a piano with purpose to learn to play it; am I too old? The piano is not yet at hand, so I am running scales on a table. Have learned the five fingering exercises, but now find some which do not conform to the fingering idea, as I have learned it. There must be some order about fingering. I live six miles in the country, and cannot go to town to find a teacher. You will oblige me greatly if you will enlighten me on this point. Is it that there is no-exact rule or order (for fingering) but all is left to the sense or wit of the learner, to finger as best he can?

"O. L. B., Nebraska."

Let me say at once you are not "too old" to learn to play the piano. People of even half your years sometimes imagine this, but your case proves they are entirely mistaken.

There is a regular fingering for scales. What is called the "C fingering" is the simplest and is used also for the scales D, E, G, and A. Scales

beginning on black keys require special fingering. In order to play a smooth, even scale, one
must learn how to slant the hand over the keys,
to pass the hand over the thumb and the thumb
under the hand, while the fingers themselves must
make free, correct up and down movements. In
the beginning the learner must pay careful attention to fingering in technical pieces, using only
the most reliable editions of music, in which the
fingering is correctly marked. Later on, when
the player understands the principles which underlie the art of fingering, he can choose one
which seems best adapted to his own hand.

In regard to the fingering of compositions,
there are certain rules and usages; these are gov-
erned by the music itself, and the touch, phrasing and interpretation required to express its
meaning.

We wish you every success in your purpose to
learn the piano.

AM I TOO OLD?

" I want your opinion on a matter of personal
interest to me. For several years I have longed
to study music; I never did so as a child. I
now go to all good concerts I can, read books
about music and composers. Before this it was
impossible for me to gratify my desire. The law
has been put upon me that I am too old; I am 23.
Will you give me your candid opinion? "

You are by no means too old to take up music
or any other study you feel inclined to. I know,

from personal knowledge, many cases where music was begun much later in life and proved a joy and delight. One was that of a young man, who never had a chance to study until he was past twenty. He is now an excellent pianist, also a teacher of ability.

You do well to hear good concerts and read good books on music. As your thought is now mature, you should be able to grasp the fundamentals much quicker than a child could possibly do. Be careful, when choosing a teacher, to select one who understands rational, foundational principles and how to develop the physical side of one's mechanism. You must learn how to relax as well as how to be firm; the right way to move fingers, wrists and arms, as well as how to count and phrase. But with industry, a love for work and for music, you will surely win.

TEACHING SCALES

" Do you approve the general custom of giving scales to first year pupils? I have not been giving them till the second year, for pupils do not know enough to play them well. Am I wrong? Then, too, is it necessary to devote so much time to scale playing? Very few pieces have long scales in them. Is there not a great deal of time wasted in poor scale playing which might better be devoted to other technical and musical work?

"D. P."

I quite agree that scales are often given too early, before the way has been prepared for them.

Some teachers think the scale is the foundation of everything, and that it is almost a crime not to start the veriest beginner on it; this seems to me the greatest mistake. There are many things to be thought of before scales are introduced. The hand must be formed, correct finger movements acquired, supple yet firm conditions established before the scale should be attempted. With an intelligent pupil, however, who practices from an hour and a half to two hours a day, all preparatory work can be done and most of the scales learned during the first year.

For scale study I do not employ the short one-octave or two-octave forms which some teachers seem so fond of. I find little use for these forms, either for fingering or for thumb or hand passing. We practice scales to gain command over the keyboard and to acquire fluency, velocity, evenness and dynamic variety. While there may not be pieces made up entirely of scale forms, yet the scale plays its part in plenty of compositions, while the keyboard facility acquired in scale practice assists in the mastery of all cadences, runs and fioriture.

WHEN TO TEACH SCALES

"I am a young teacher, just starting out. Many questions perplex me at present. I should like to ask when beginners should be taught the scales? I have heard teachers say they begin them at the first lesson; others do not give them for a year. Which is right?"

Do not think of starting your instruction to a beginner with scale playing; it would only be time wasted. You must teach a hundred things first. Hand position, finger action, single tones and pairs of tones, then simple exercises through the hand; after which you can gradually prepare for the scale by training the thumb to move quickly under the hand, and the latter to be carried smoothly over the thumb. Before all this is acquired, however, you can explain the scale plan quite simply to the pupil, who can then play any scale you name, by using a single finger, combined with rotary arm movement.

SCALE PLAYING

" In one of the current musical magazines some one offers rules for scale playing which are contrary to my ideas and to the way I have been teaching scales. So I am referring the matter to you, as you always make things so plain.

"The writer says: ' Arms should be held close to the sides. . . . Keep wrists in horizontal position, with hand, or a little higher (!) Arms should be horizontal with the keyboard, or a little higher (!) '

"Are the above rules correct? E. D."

The rules you quote are certainly *not* correct, not in this enlightened day, when we are becoming awake to the causes back of good scale playing, and the fundamental principles of hand position. They might have been considered correct half a century ago; therefore the writer is probably an elderly man, who has not kept up with the times. It is the bane of our profession that we seem to be, both in teaching and in writing, still under the yoke of pernicious "rules," at variance with the true principles of things.

You may think me severe. Let us look more closely at the rules you have quoted and see. "Arms should be held close to the sides." How under Heaven is this possible, if one play a four or five octave scale? A tyro would know better. Perhaps the inventor of the rules requires merely a one octave scale, played in the center of the keyboard. In no other way can arms be held close to the sides.

"Keep wrists on level with hands or a little higher." Another old time rule, long since out of date. High wrists in scale playing generally mean stiff wrists. It is the same with high arms, only worse. Stiff arms in scale playing ruin the scale.

The writer of the rules omits all of the fundamental principles. He has nothing to say about the hand being held in scale relation, that is in a slanting position across the keys; nothing about passing hand over the thumb or thumb under the hand; nothing about forward movement or backward movement, as well as a few other important matters. If you have been well taught yourself, you must understand these points. You also know the arm must hang free from the shoulder, able to move backward and forward as the scale requires. You know that, as fingers act from the knuckle joint, the wrist must be held *lower* than the knuckles and must be adjusted to the movement of the arm. Arms are not to be held higher than the keyboard, but rather *lower,* and their natural weight is suspended on the finger tips, when mezzo power is used. If all young teachers will be faithful in pointing the way, presenting and inculcating correct principles of scale playing, there will be many more good players among us than there are now — many more who understand what ought to be done and are learning to do it.

THE ARM IN PLAYING

"I have recently seen this statement in print: 'Arm technic should be reserved for the intermediate or advanced stage of piano study.' Is this the right idea? I had not supposed it was. I shall be glad of your opinion."

No, it is not right; it belongs to the dark ages of piano study, when the value of arm movements was not understood — that is by the rank and file of teachers and players. We now know that arm weight and the ability to use the arm correctly and with freedom, gives depth and beauty to the tone. Shall this beauty of tone be only permitted the advanced player? Must those lower down be condemned to use only finger action, with stiff arms; must they be deprived of the knowledge of how to cultivate arm movements till they become advanced players? If this course be followed they will never become advanced.

No, pupils correctly taught learn arm movements in their earliest lessons. Arm technic is cultivated along with finger technic; both grow together. Thus the player is trained on all sides and learns correct conditions from the start.

Teachers must understand principles underlying correct and beautiful tone production, also the difference between necessary and unnecessary movements. Then they will be able to refute foolish ideas advanced by some writers and teachers. At no time has this definite knowledge been so necessary as at the present moment, when so much is said and written about teaching and playing, which means very little in the right direction and very much in the wrong. Let us all study the principles and base our work upon them; then we can uncover these errors that are abroad; then we can let our light shine, because we know the right and can spread it abroad.

DISHONEST PUPILS

"I am writing to ask if anything can be done in the following case: A young man came to me to arrange for piano lessons: He knew my work and seemed anxious to place himself in my hands. I told him I never accepted a pupil for fewer than ten lessons to start with. He assured me he wished to continue indefinitely; in short his aim was to become a good pianist. He found my terms satisfactory, only stipulating he might be allowed to pay by the lesson. He came and took one lesson. As his technic was very faulty,

I showed him many exercises for fingers, hands
and arms, which would be of greatest benefit to
him in every way. I felt the lesson must have
been an illumination, as he was very ignorant
of technical principles, had never memorized a
note of music in his life and knew little of piano
literature. I became interested in him and made
the lesson longer than agreed; I also loaned him
a book on piano technic. The next week, just
before lesson hour, an untidy postal written in
pencil arrived, saying the pupil would not continue lessons. Now I call this rank dishonesty,
and think his name should be made public, as a
warning to others.

"Will you advise me as to whether I handled
this case discreetly? Why should the seemingly
anxious pupil suddenly turn to a dishonest one?
Was the fault with me?

"M. J."

From what you write and what I know of
your work, I think you were conscientious and
tried to give the new pupil a solid foundation.
The trouble evidently was, though pretending to
be serious, he was far from being so. He really
wanted only superficial instruction. If you had
agreed to give him nothing but pieces he would
have continued his lessons. He was probably a
trifler and it is better to be rid of such.

However; from a business point of view, you
made two errors. When he came and agreed to
start with ten lessons, you should have had that
in contract, with his signature. Secondly, you

should have exacted payment for at least five lessons in advance. In the first instance, if he had the intention of being dishonest, he would be so whether he signed a paper or not. But, with the money paid, he would not be likely to throw up his contract. No teacher of reputation, able to show good results, should be judged by one lesson, simply because his ideas are new to the pupil. If a pupil comes to a teacher of reputation and wide experience, he must trust the teacher long enough to test his method of teaching. Ten lessons should be the shortest period for which a capable teacher should accept a pupil. No reputable school would permit such action on the part of a pupil, as you describe. Why not have a printed form of contract, in which you agree to teach Mr.— for ten weeks, and he agrees to study with you for that length of time. He must sign this paper with full name and address, also giving references, if a stranger to you. This would at least be some safeguard.

These forms of dishonesty should be stamped out. For there are many kinds from which teachers of music suffer; from the pupil who engages one's best hour "for the season," then leaves in the middle of the year, for no valid reason — to the pupil who wants to pay by the lesson, and is frequently absent. Competent piano teachers must stand up for their rights and conduct their business affairs on a business basis. Rather refuse outright the pupil who will not come up to reasonable terms than to accept such a one and find him, or her, a continual thorn in the flesh.

WEAK FINGER-JOINTS

"I am troubled about a certain condition of my hand, and that is the weakness of the nail joint of my fingers. If I try to play with any power, these joints cave in and are very unsteady. I have played the piano for a number of years without ever noticing this condition, as my early teachers never said anything about it. As I read and learn more in regard to hand position and condition, I gradually realize the weakness of my fingers and locate the trouble at the nail joint. Will you give me some advice in the matter?

"H. K., Nebraska."

That you have discovered the weakness of your fingers shows you are awake and thinking along the right lines. It *is* necessary to cultivate firmness in the shaping joints of the fingers, no matter what your present teacher may tell you. Leschetizky, one of the greatest teachers of the piano, required rock-like firmness of the nail-joint, and he formed some of the greatest pianists of our time. He strongly insisted on this point; it was one of the few absolute principles he laid down. For, while he disclaimed having a cut-and-dried "method," he averred his only method consisted of loose wrists and arms, arched hands and firm fingers.

The beginner, rightly taught, learns at once to arch the hand, to cultivate freedom and elasticity of knuckles and firmness of fingers. Much of this can be taught at a table. He begins at the table to try the strength of his fingers by putting a gentle pressure on them; the pressure being increased as fingers grow stronger, learn to resist the weight and "stand up" under it.

If you wish to overcome this weakness in your own hand, why not put yourself through a drill, dropping difficult pieces for a time, until your hand is in better condition to master them. You may discover other faults and weaknesses which you had not noticed and which need to be eliminated.

It is very beneficial to have a renovating period for one's technic, to give the playing mechanism an overhauling. The owner of a fine piece of machinery keeps it well oiled and in perfect repair. Just so the pianist must see that his technical machine is kept in perfect condition, in order that it will give the best service.

A QUESTION OF "LOOSE" KNUCKLES

"Consequent from much experimentation, I must conclude, in my personal case, that one of the most important conditions in the production of a beautiful, mellow tone, is the relaxation of looseness of the knuckle joints. Leschetizky gives many good principles of tone production, yet I do not recall that he ever mentions looseness of the knuckle joints as necessary to tone production. Do you not think it very necessary? I play with arched hand position; is it not possible to maintain an arched hand, loose wrists,

firm fingers and *loose* knuckles all at the same
time? I should appreciate your ideas concern-
ing the above.

" R. M., North Car."

The point you raise is not quite clear. You
ask if it is not possible to play with arched hand,
firm fingers and yet loose knuckle joints. If by
looseness of knuckle-joints you mean the necessary flexibility and capacity for quick, easy movement, I answer it is possible to have all these conditions present at once. If, however, by looseness, you mean flabbiness or caving in of the
knuckles, under pressure, this is certainly not
desirable, nor is it compatible with firm fingers
and arched hand. To me this would seem an
impossibility. For, if the knuckles are so loose
as to lose their back-bone and shape, the hand
cannot preserve its arched position. Neither can
a tone with any resonance or power be produced. Soft tones only would be possible.

It is quite true Leschetizky never advocated
loose knuckles in the sense of caving in or flabby
joints; but he approved of absolutely controlled
flexibility of the knuckle-joints, otherwise how
would it be possible to move fingers with exactness and swiftness?

STRAIGHTENED FINGERS

" So many beginners seem to have the fault of
straightening the fingers on the keys. This position lowers the back of the hand and throws
the thumb quite a distance away from the key-

board. When the thumb has to play, a jerk is required to bring it up to its key. How can I correct this fault?   H. L., Penna."

The beginner's hand should first be trained at a table before he is taken to the piano. At the table he learns to form the hand in arched position, with rounded fingers. Simple exercises for finger action are also executed at the table, so that when the pupil plays them at the piano the fingers are already accustomed to the curved position. The teacher must be ever on the watch to see that a correct position of hand is maintained. Eternal vigilance seems to be the price of good hand position and proper finger action. Fortunately, some pupils adopt the arched hand position readily, even naturally. The teacher draws a sigh of relief when working with such pupils.

SELF EDUCATION

" I am afraid my questions will be somewhat different from the usual inquiries, but I shall be very grateful if you will answer.

1. To what extent do you consider it possible for a student to educate himself in music?

2. Is it possible for one who has received but little musical instruction, to learn the works of the great masters, if he has but little or no money to pay for lessons?

3. Is it not strange that there are night schools, where one may receive instruction in almost any subject, yet there is nothing in this line for music, the most beautiful study of all?

4. Would you consider the following list of studies and books a good one to develop technic, or are there better ones? (I have none of them, but as far as I can judge from articles in musical magazines, they are the best.)

Czerny, Selected Studies, Liebling, Op. 740.

Czerny, Op. 740, Nineteen Etudes, Unschuld.

Presser, School of Octaves and Arpeggios.

Pinter, School of Octaves.

Cramer-Bulow, 50 Selected Studies.

Duvernoy, Etudes, Op. 120.

Bach, Well Tempered Clavichord, and Inventions.

When a child I lived on the prairie in Nebraska, fifteen miles from any town. Practically all the instruction I ever received was sixteen lessons on the piano during the summer months, from two teachers at the Conservatory in Lincoln. The most difficult piece I ever had was The Butterfly, by Merkel. Since coming to Oregon, I have had no piano, but took some violin lessons on a borrowed violin. The study of the violin helped me a great deal with my piano study. I have a piano now, and have been trying to practice alone, but I need a whole year or more of thorough technical work. I try my best to study alone, but have come to the place where I make no headway, and am getting careless of fingering and other things. Do you think it too late to take up music seriously? I am 23.

C. I. B.,
Oregon."

I am a firm believer in studying music at any age whatever. It is never too late to take up music seriously; I have known people of 75 or 80 who have begun to study, and have found great pleasure and profit in it. In your case it would not be beginning, but rather continuing, as you already play some and have a good natural touch.

1. I am sure you can do a great deal for yourself in technic, as well as in other ways. Take account of your stock of knowledge; see what you already know and consider what you need to know. In what condition is your technic? Do you produce a clear, round tone? Is it expressive and capable of both power and delicacy? Have you any velocity? Test yourself on these points. Do you know all the keys, major and minor, with the chords and scales for each key? Have you studied chords and octaves on the piano? How are your trills, scales and arpeggios? If you are to teach yourself, you must make a small outlay for the necessary music and books.

2. Along with your technic study, get a little insight into Bach. An edition of his small pieces edited by MacDowell, is very interesting; they will make a delightful beginning. After them comes the Gavottes and Gigues and some of the Inventions. A few of the Mendelssohn Songs without Words would be a good contrast to the polyphonic character of Bach's music. Begin Beethoven with the Sonatines, Op. 49, and the

Bagatelles, Op. 33, and Chopin with the Pre-ludes.

3. It is indeed strange that the public schools cannot do as much for music as for other studies. Perhaps, in time, those in authority will wake up to the value of music as an educational force. Why can we not have night schools for music? I am sure they would be a success, if rightly handled.

4. In regard to books of studies, those you mention are all good. The Duvernoy would come first, before using others on your list.

FROM A SELF-TAUGHT STUDENT

1. How long or how often should one practice finger exercises?

2. When should one leave a theme or exercise and pass on to another?

3. When and how often should one learn pieces?

4. How can one tell which grade of piece he may properly play?

My method is that of Lebert and Stark, and I am studying without a teacher. If you will add a word of advice I shall be grateful.

H. W. L.

It is always pleasant to hear from those who love music so much they struggle to teach themselves, if unable to employ a teacher.

1. You need daily practice in finger exercises. The time given to them depends on the amount you devote to study. From a quarter to a third

can be given to technic, including études. If you practice three hours, devote one to technical study.

2. If we practice such fundamental things as trills, scales, arpeggios, chords and octaves, we never really leave them as finished, for with constant practice we learn to do them more perfectly, with greater velocity and smoothness, with more variety of touch and tone. When we have learned these forms and principles in the key of C, for instance, they are to be studied in every other key, major and minor. In regard to study material, you might enjoy the "Graded Course," which Mrs. Crosby Adams has laid out in seven books, beginning with simple études and small pieces and going on to advanced musicianship. The careful practice of Heller Selected Studies, together with the easier Sonatas and Sonatinas, will be most helpful and yield good results.

3. Always have one piece on hand, on which you are concentrating. When you feel you can play it correctly as to notes, phrasing, fingering and tempo, take up another, always keeping the former one in practice. Use metronome to determine whether or not you can reach the required tempo, although the marks for tempo are often faulty in poor editions. Get the best editions possible, to avoid these errors.

It is a good plan to try out the piece just memorized on your family or intimate friend to make sure you can play it correctly.

HOW SHALL I ESTABLISH MYSELF IN A MUSIC CENTER?

" I live in a small city, where I have been teaching music for several years with considerable success and have a large class of pupils. But this place is dead, musically. We have very few concerts during the season. When I read of the great advantages of a music center like New York, I grow very restive over remaining here and want to branch out. What are my chances of making a living there? Can you advise me?

"N. C."

Many are asking the same question and it is one very difficult to answer. There are two important items to consider,— the Field and Yourself. I can only give you a thought on each.

The Field here is crowded with those teaching piano, also those establishing themselves as accompanists. You wish to do both. Some of the greatest teachers of the world are here; many foreign artists, too, who intend to stay. There are thousands of teachers here, but there is always room at the bottom for one to work up. One must be in some way notable, either as performer or instructor, to awaken interest and secure early recognition. One's name must be somewhat known, or one must have a circle of friends who can help. Far be it from me to discourage any one from making the attempt; but you must go into it with open eyes, clearly aware of the difficulties.

Yourself. What you are yourself — what you have in you — makes all the difference in the world. As I do not know you personally, I cannot tell what you can do. If a young girl, or young woman, asks advice about establishing herself in this metropolis, as you have done, and I know her to be small, shy, diffident, with no personality, no push, of very modest musical attainments, not a fine pianist and quite unknown in the world of music, would it be right and just, think you, for any one to make light of the lions in the way, and urge her to come to this great city, in which thousands of the profession are fighting for existence? Even though she has taught in her home town for several years, with considerable success. That fact of itself is not enough to establish her in New York.

I should say to her: If you have a number of influential friends, who believe in you, and on whom you can depend to work for and help you secure pupils, then take the opportunity and be grateful for the fortunate chance. Otherwise, by all means stay where you are, you will be much better off. My advice would be: Keep on studying, use your vacations for study, seek to perfect yourself in every way, and when the time is ripe and you are ready for it, the way will surely be opened.

On the other hand, if you are a competent teacher, with considerable experience in handling pupils and situations, used to meeting people, able to talk and express yourself well, to explain with conviction your manner of teaching, able to hold your own and take the initiative, with plenty of grit and push, good humor and tact, your chances are much more promising. Best of all, if you are a good pianist, you can introduce yourself through a couple of invitation recitals. There are several ways to do this: through a music, or department store; or, if you are able to meet the expense, you can give a recital in one of the concert halls. It may be you could first secure opportunity as an accompanist, by visiting the vocal teachers, who are often in need of a good player who understands this branch of the work. Influential friends are now — as always — of greatest possible assistance in opening the way and introducing a new comer. But everything in the end still depends on yourself, what you are and what you can do. People have come to New York entirely unheralded and unknown, who by sheer force of talent and grit, have won out in a couple of years, or even in one year. Others have taken much longer to arrive, although they have started in well equipped. *It all depends.* You are bound to succeed if you keep at it long enough and have the right stuff in you. It means plenty of hard work and never yielding to discouragements, no matter how trying or crushing they may appear. The right kind of effort always pays in the end.

A word about getting started as accompanist. Do not think, because you play the piano reasonably well, accompanying must be easy. On the contrary, it is often more difficult to play a satisfactory accompaniment than to render an instrumental solo. In a solo the player is free — can do what he likes as to tempo, phrasing, interpretation. When playing for another he is no longer free to follow his own wishes, for he must play as the soloist wishes. At the same time he must be the backbone, the mainstay, the support of the singer. He should neither follow nor lead, but be absolutely with the singer. He must be equal to any emergency, for no one can tell beforehand what the singer may do. She may take liberties, leave out whole sections of the piece. No matter, the player must be with her every time. She may at the last moment, as she steps upon the platform, wish the song transposed. There is no time to think out the new key, it must be done on the spot.

It will be seen the accompanist must possess good technic, read well, transpose at sight, have keen intelligence, sympathy and great presence of mind. Success in accompanying is the result of hard work, plus tact and resource. It can be won on those terms.

for each other and for me. When they can play
a group of pieces with ease and without mistakes, let them appear before some competent
musicians who are able to pass on their merits.
If they endure this ordeal, they will have much
more confidence and be more willing to play in
a larger way; but don't rush them before the
public until they have had some such preparation, for it injures both them and you.

"I think teachers should do much more for
the preparation of their pupils for public playing than they do. The best way is to have a
criticism class every week. It is because the
standards of the teachers are often so low that
little is expected of the pupil."

I could not but be impressed by the wide experience and common sense view the Professor
took of the subject. I determined, if ever I got
through with the present Commencement Musi-
cale alive, I would work along quite different
lines in the future.

TREATMENT OF THE PUPILS

A colleague of mine, well up in the profession,
called to see me late one afternoon, and we soon
fell to discussing the absorbing topic of ways and
means. My friend is an American pianist and
teacher of very pronounced ideas — together with
the artistic temperament. As he held forth on
the management of pupils, the thought occurred
to me — what good fun it would be to take him to

the Professor, and let them argue it out together; while I, as silent listener, would get the benefit of their conclusions.

I knew the Professor was at leisure at this hour, so we proceeded down the corridor to his rooms, entered, and were soon chatting comfortably.

The Professor was in an extremely placid mood and I wondered in what spirit he would listen to a discussion. To start them going, I said:

"Here is a man who has come to the place where he can pick and choose. If he feels he cannot get along with a pupil, he will have nothing to do with her. If a pupil plays the same wrong note three lessons running, he sends her off."

The Professor regarded my friend as though he were a new genus; then he remarked calmly:

"Patience is the greatest virtue a teacher can possess and some of us are long sighted enough to try and cultivate it. I tell you, boys, it's one of your best assets. Patience, joined to a kindness and courtesy, will fill up your teaching lists and your pockets at the same time. Impatience never attracts pupils, neither does sarcasm.

"When I was studying in Germany in early days," he continued, "I saw so much of this drastic treatment of students, by irascible foreign masters, that I determined, when my turn came to teach, I would turn the other way round and win the pupil by kindness. Besides, Amer-

ican pupils will not endure such belaboring —
they are too high spirited."

"But, Professor," began my friend, "perhaps
you don't know how trying pupils can be: some
of them are more than the artistic temperament
of the teacher can stand."

"Don't I know how trying they can be? Hundreds upon hundreds of them have passed
through my hands; yet with it all I believe most
of them are my friends to this day. I make it
my business to be their friend — to take an interest in them. I try not merely to cram my
wisdom into them, but to draw out what they
have, and see what I can make of them.

"Another thing. Pupils come to us to be
taught, to get all the help possible. It is our
business to give it, without stint; they pay us for
it, and it's up to us to help them. Everybody has
some degree of aptitude for music, and it's our
province to find out in what direction it lies —
to nurture it and make it bud and blossom.
We must try and make promising pupils out of
unpromising ones. As for the teacher's 'artistic
temperament,' well — if we go off the handle for
an occasional wrong note, we had better not try
to teach music for a living.

"Now, I talk severely to my pupils at times,
to spur them on to greater effort, or to wake them
up, if they are lazy. But I make them see there
is no personal animosity, only my deep interest
in their progress. As for turning them off for a

couple of wrong notes, I should never think of it.

"Be assured there is no profession or calling which needs so much patience, tact and kindness as that of teaching music; the sooner teachers realize this fact the better for all concerned.

"However, I do not need to preach to such efficient members of the profession as yourselves," the Professor rose with his genial smile. "If we are to attend that recital, I suppose we must be on the way," and he bowed us out politely.

ENROLLMENT DAY

It is Enrollment Day at the University of Music where the Professor holds sway. It is his duty to interview and examine all candidates, appointing them to the various teachers as he thinks best.

He is just about to begin his task; the anteroom is already nearly filled with would-be students; they will be sent for, one at a time; after the ordeal they will pass out through an opposite door. Let us place ourselves in an obscure corner and listen awhile to what happens in the studio.

The Professor starts the day in a calm, magnanimous frame of mind; this condition may vary, and is not likely to last through the day.

A young lady enters, very fashionably dressed. She explains she has taken lessons a long time; Professor Thunder was her last teacher; she hands a copy of her "piece" to the examiner, then seats herself at the piano, after screwing

up the piano stool as high as it will go. Her
piece is one of the Scherzos of Chopin. She at-
tacks it pêle mêle, with pedal down, plays as fast
and as loud as possible, with plenty of wrong
notes into the bargain.

The Professor soon calls a halt.

"Will you tell me, young lady," he says in his
bland tones, "what key this piece is written in,
what time signature stands at the beginning
and also why you keep the pedal down all the
time?"

She gazes at him in astonishment, then she
laughs. "I guess I was nervous and forgot the
pedal."

"Perhaps; but you may answer my other questions as to key and meter."

But she couldn't. Then he says:

"I will try your ear and see what kind of tone
sense you have."

"Oh, I never studied that; I only learned
piano."

"Ah, I see," assents the Professor and writes
something in his note-book. The young lady may
be disappointed with the result of her examination when she comes to take her first lesson.
She passes out the other door.

The next candidate said she wanted to become
a teacher of music. To this end she had attended
a six weeks' summer course at a conservatory
and received a certificate. Having several
months to spare before beginning her work as
teacher, she had concluded to take a few finish-

ing lessons under the Professor's guidance.

The Professor scrutinizes her rather sharply as he glances at the roll of music she hands him. Then he remarks:

"Suppose, instead of playing these Rhapsodies of Liszt and Brahms you have here, you do some scales." He busies himself winding and setting the metronome.

A frightened look comes into the girl's eyes, but she seats herself and begins.

Ye gods! The scale of C, quarter notes at 120, is too much for her; such a mess as she makes of it — everything wrong, even to the fingering. She looks up helplessly at the Professor, whose wrath is rising.

"You mean to say," he exclaims, "that you expect to *teach* music when you can't even play the scale of C? Preposterous! How can you show others what you can't do yourself?"

"I have never used the metronome — it puts me out," she pleads.

"Play without it then, but play the scale of B," directs the Professor.

But it was all worse than before. A few other tests are made, and then the discomfited pupil withdraws.

The girl who follows enters with a self-satisfied air, and introduces herself as a pupil of one of the most admired artists before the public, whose name need not be divulged. With him she had studied interpretation; he had told her "so

many interesting things," and his lessons were
"so illuminating."

The Professor didn't seem as greatly impressed
as she had expected. He is hard-hearted enough
to ask for some chords in various positions, first
piano, then *mezzo* and afterwards *fortissimo.*

Of course she can't do them; she had probably
never practiced chords outside of pieces in her
life, so she makes a sorry spectacle, with her
floundering attempts. It gets on the Professor's
nerves and he begins to pace up and down the
floor.

"What possessed you to go to an artist-
teacher; why didn't you go to a pedagogue and
learn something?" he bursts out. "You don't
know the first principles of piano technic!"

And so it goes on. Why had not these appli-
cants studied scales, chords and principles before
they came? Better ask why they had not learned
piano playing correctly from the foundation up.
Yet in spite of their inefficiency, they all wanted
the veneer of finishing lessons with an artist-
teacher.

The Professor's patience was wearing thread-
bare.

At last a pleasant looking girl enters. Her
slender, pliant form, round white arms and
shapely hands, the bright eyes and fresh color
in her cheeks betokened vigorous health. You
felt at once those hands could produce ringing
tones from the instrument, and so it proved.

For when the Professor demands scales, she is equal to them, playing in various rhythms and in almost any tempo. The Professor regards her first with astonishment then with approbation. It was as sunshine after a storm to hear such beautiful technic.

"Now, play me something," he said.

"Shall it be Bach?" asks the girl.

Receiving assent, she plunges into one of the Toccatas. She plays it brilliantly, effectively, with rich, full tone and a fine appreciation of its many beauties.

"Who has taught you?" exclaims the Professor, as the splendid final chords die away and the girl sits quietly awaiting his verdict.

"Only Mr. V——."

"My pupil! He has done good work. You are the only girl I've seen to-day who knows what she's about; and you didn't get it from an artist-teacher,— with an unpronounceable name — or any other name,— either. Come to my class next week, and prepare the first movement of Schumann's G minor Sonata, if you have not yet studied it."

THE PROFESSOR HITS OUT

The Professor sprang to his feet and began pacing the studio. He thrust his hands behind him, a way he has when ruffled. The Professor is usually sweet tempered except when excited over some wrongdoing, then is not quite accountable for his tongue. When he detects pretense and sham he is apt to hit out right and left.

I had stopped in after my lessons, and found him in this state of mind, the cause of which was a note he had received. His usually genial smile had vanished and a frown puckered his forehead. He brought his clenched fist *sforzando* on the table to emphasize his words.

"No, sir, no one can make me believe a so-called artist-teacher — a so-called, if you please, can really earn his forty dollars an hour, or even his twenty-five. Do you know what that means per minute? No one has any business to ask such sums. And what can he put into each minute that will be really worth the outlay?"

"Oh, Professor, isn't that a bit mercenary?"

"On the part of the artist-teacher? Yes, I quite agree with you," he answered, ignoring my obvious meaning. "Those teachers come here — foreigners of course — and for this very reason, if for no other, we bow down to them, and are ready to pay them anything they ask. They, on their part, seem to have no conscience, no fellow feeling, no artistic sympathy. All they seem to care for is to accumulate gold — gold. And this in a country that pours out lavishly to patronize their concerts and lauds them personally to the skies. They are fêted and honored everywhere; in return they do — what? Just fleece the poor students and young teachers. Oh, it makes me hot around the collar, whenever I think of it."

"The students need not go to these great

names," I put in rather feebly, just for the sake of answering. In my innermost consciousness I felt the Professor was nine-tenths right.

"No, they need not; but we are so crazy over here, that the young ones think if they can get a few lessons with Mr. B. or Mr. G., it will put them on the high road to fame and fortune. They even think one lesson will work wonders. Bah, what can one learn in one lesson!

"I remember, as a boy, having the same foolish dreams myself. I took one of the less familiar Liszt Rhapsodies — over which I had been working more than a year, and went to a well-known pianist, who was then giving recitals in New York. No one, in those days, thought of asking over five dollars a lesson. The artist heard me play the piece, then he read it through for me — he was not familiar with it himself — and that's all I got for my five dollars. I remember to this day how well he read at sight. Perhaps it was worth the money to see how he did it. But if he had asked me twenty-five or forty dollars, as is done now, I should have said, 'No, thank you, you can keep your high-priced knowledge.' It meant enough privation to give up that five dollars anyway."

"What has excited you so, Professor?" I asked when he halted for breath.

"Oh, this has been in my mind a long time, but just now I had a note from one of my pupils. Knowing I had to be away a few weeks, she had asked permission to go to Mr. G. to play for him certain pieces he makes a specialty of. She wrote him, and found she must take ten lessons, at twenty dollars each. Of course she will not do it. This is only one case; there are many others I could mention.

"If these prices were only charged the rich, who can well pay; but it is the poor who always have to pay — if they can. They are the ones who should be helped and encouraged, by granting them reduced rates."

"Bravo, Professor! I think your head is level on this subject. I wish the sensible teachers could all stand together and fight these soaring prices. It seems to me six — eight or at the very outside, ten dollars is all a teacher can really earn at the present time, even though he has the greatest gift for imparting, plus the finest method in the world. But the sad fact is, the artist-teacher has little or no method of any kind. He is not a real teacher anyway, for he seldom can tell *how* to do things. If the student is already an artist, they can meet on equal ground and talk things over. Then the time can be spent pleasantly in each other's company. Why the younger artist should hand over forty dollars for this exchange of views does not seem fair. You agree, Professor?"

"Indeed my boy, you are pretty near right. I have fought a good many evils and abuses in the music and teaching business and I intend to do all I can against this one. In the meantime," he added, with a return of amiability, "come out with me, I want to show you a picture I have just seen."

He drew my arm in his and together we left the studio.

THE PROFESSOR HITS OUT AGAIN

The Professor's door stood slightly ajar. I could hear his rapid strides within, and thought it would be good fun to see what was the trouble. I cautiously pushed the door open a trifle further; the Professor caught sight of me.

"Come in, come in, my boy," he called out. "You are a good safety valve, as I have found on several occasions. Just hear this."

"What is the matter this time, Professor? Has some one been treading on your toes?"

A current musical periodical lay open on his desk; he went over and took it up.

"Here is an interview with a man who has made himself famous as a pianist; he is known all over the world. He avers here that there is no such thing as a perfectly even scale, and if there were, it would be deadly monotonous. In fact he has no use for scales anyhow, and does not advise studying them. He may mean all this in a far-fetched, psychological sense, but the average pupil is not going to put such a fine point on it. He will say: 'Why should I try so hard to make each finger independent, to render my touch even and dependable, so that I can play smooth, flowing, even scales and passages? My teacher insists on this, saying these things are

absolutely necessary, if I would become even a re-
spectable player. But here is Mr. —, one of the
greatest lights in the pianistic world; he says one
doesn't need to do them. Whom shall, I believe — the professor or the artist? The Professor's way is much harder; he keeps me at work
all the time to perfect my technic. The way of
the pianist is far easier, and as he has made a
world-wide success, I think I'll follow him.' You
see how it works?

"He says, too," continued my friend, resum-
ing his rapid walk; "'I do not believe in so-
called piano technic, which must be laboriously
practiced outside of pieces.' Now, what do you
think of that? How can any sane man say such
things? Here I am, working night and day to
train a small army of students and teachers who
shall understand principles of technic, from an
educational standpoint; who shall be thoroughly
grounded in technic and be able to apply these
principles in their study and performance of
pieces. And now, here comes along a man who
says all this is not necessary. What will my
pupils think; what will the pupils of other
conscientious and painstaking masters think?
Such opinions do a great deal of harm to the
profession, to the business of teaching and learning — to the cause of thorough education in
music."

"But my dear sir," I said, "I am sure the
artist in question has no desire to work harm
to either student, teacher, or to the cause of

musical education. The whole trouble lies in the fact that he is a pianist and not a musical educator."

The Professor halted and threw me one of his flashing smiles.

" Ah, my boy, you see it too — that is just the reason. People have said to me this artist is only posing when he makes these remarks; I won't accuse him of that either. He's an idealist, who loves free speech and likes to be different from everybody else. He likes to shock us into attention. All the same it's an awful pity. It may be he doesn't know or care how he holds his hands on the piano; shall all learners imitate such anarchy? Shall they all turn away from all principles which we are trying to instill into them? I am just as positive as that I stand here that it is because my students are well grounded in foundational principles and developed along those lines, that they do good work, love their music and are able to interpret understandingly; also that my teachers can secure good school positions anywhere. Those of my students who are working along in the right groove are known wherever they go as examples of what my teaching can give."

" Yes, indeed, Professor," I answered heartily, " you do splendid work, and have turned out some wonderfully fine musicians — real artists."

" Where do you think they would be if I had not insisted on a thorough technical foundation?

It takes a strong head and hand to manage gifted pupils, for they are too apt to fancy thorough training is quite unnecessary. The pianist in question is so gifted that he plays beautifully in spite of the handicap of insufficient technical preparation, although, if the real truth were known, he, too, had to work at scales and technic in the very beginning. My contention is, that now having reached such a high pinnacle, he should not spread these wrong ideas, and make the rest of us all this trouble to correct them — if we ever can!"

"Don't worry about that, dear Professor, for your work always speaks for itself; you are certainly fulfilling your mission and many will rise up to call you blessed."

"Thanks, my boy,— you are a famous safety valve," and with a hearty laugh he slapped me on the back. "Now go," he added, pushing me gently out; "I've no end of work to do before I leave here."

THE END

3 1197 00116 9082